How To Use This Study Guide

This ten-lesson study guide corresponds to *"How Close Are We to the End?"* with *Rick Renner* (Renner TV). Each lesson in this study guide covers a topic that is addressed during the program series, with questions and references supplied to draw you deeper into your own private study of the Scriptures on this subject.

To derive the most benefit from this study guide, consider the following:

First, watch or listen to the program prior to working through the corresponding lesson in this guide. (Programs can also be viewed at **renner.org** by clicking on the Media/Archives links or on our Renner Ministries YouTube channel.)

Second, take the time to look up the scriptures included in each lesson. Prayerfully consider their application to your own life.

Third, use a journal or notebook to make note of your answers to each lesson's Study Questions and Practical Application challenges.

Fourth, invest specific time in prayer and in the Word of God to consult with the Holy Spirit. Write down the scriptures or insights He reveals to you.

Finally, take action! Whatever the Lord tells you to do according to His Word, do it.

For added insights on this subject, it is recommended that you obtain Rick Renner's book *Signs You'll See Just Before Jesus Comes*. You may also select from Rick's other available resources by placing your order at **renner.org** or by calling 1-800-742-5593.

LESSON 1

TOPIC
The Signs of His Coming

SCRIPTURES
1. **Matthew 24:1-3** — And Jesus went out, and departed from the temple: and his disciples came to him for to shew him the buildings of the temple. And Jesus said unto them, See ye not all these things? verily I say unto you, There shall not be left here one stone upon another, that shall not be thrown down. And as he sat upon the mount of Olives, the disciples came unto him privately, saying, Tell us, when shall these things be? and what shall be the sign of thy coming, and of the end of the world?
2. **Matthew 24:36** — But of that day and hour knoweth no man, no, not the angels of heaven, but my Father only.
3. **John 16:13** — Howbeit when he, the Spirit of truth, is come, he will guide you into all truth: for he shall not speak of himself; but whatsoever he shall hear, that shall he speak: and he will shew you things to come.

GREEK WORDS
1. "when" — ποτέ (*pote*): exactly when; indicates specific information
2. "what" — τι (*ti*): minute, miniscule detail; exactly; explicitly
3. "sign" — σημεῖον (*semeion*): a marker or sign used to alert a traveler to where he is on a road; authenticating marks or specific signs
4. "coming" — παρουσία (*parousia*): to be present; a technical expression for the royal visit of a king or emperor; the arrival of one who alone has the authority to deal with a situation and put things in correct order
5. "end" — συντέλειας (*sunteleias*): the closure, the summation, or wrap-up of the age
6. "world" — αἰῶνος (*aionos*): not the world itself, but the age

A Note From Rick Renner

I am on a personal quest to see a "revival of the Bible" so people can establish their lives on a firm foundation that will stand strong and endure the test as end-time storm winds begin to intensify.

In order to experience a revival of the Bible in your personal life, it is important to take time each day to read, receive, and apply its truths to your life. James tells us that if we will continue in the perfect law of liberty — refusing to be forgetful hearers, but determined to be doers — we will be blessed in our ways. As you watch or listen to the programs in this series and work through this corresponding study guide, I trust you will search the Scriptures and allow the Holy Spirit to help you hear something new from God's Word that applies specifically to your life. I encourage you to be a doer of the Word He reveals to you. Whatever the cost, I assure you — it will be worth it.

> Thy words were found, and I did eat them;
> and thy word was unto me the joy and rejoicing of mine heart:
> for I am called by thy name, O Lord God of hosts.
> — Jeremiah 15:16

Your brother and friend in Jesus Christ,

Rick Renner

Unless otherwise indicated, all scripture quotations are taken from the *King James Version* of the Bible.

Scripture quotations marked (*AMPC*) are taken from the *Amplified® Bible, Classic Edition*. Copyright © 1954, 1958, 1962, 1964, 1965, 1987 by The Lockman Foundation. Used by permission. **www.Lockman.org**.

Scripture references marked (*J.B. Phillips*) are taken from *The New Testament in Modern English* by J.B. Phillips copyright © 1960, 1972 J. B. Phillips. Administered by The Archbishops' Council of the Church of England. Used by Permission.

Scripture quotations marked (*MSG*) are taken from *The Message*, copyright © 1993, 2002, 2018 by Eugene H. Peterson. Used by permission of NavPress. All rights reserved. Represented by Tyndale House Publishers, Inc.

Scripture quotations marked (*NKJV*) are taken from the *New King James Version®*. Copyright © 1982 by Thomas Nelson. Used by permission. All rights reserved.

Scripture quotations marked (*NLT*) are taken from the Holy Bible, *New Living Translation*, copyright © 1996, 2004, 2015 by Tyndale House Foundation. Used by permission of Tyndale House Publishers, Inc., Carol Stream, Illinois 60188. All rights reserved.

Scriptures quoted from the *Renner Interpretive Version®* (*RIV*) copyrighted © 2020, 2024 by Teaching You Can Trust, LLC, and published by Harrison House Publishers. Used by permission. Renner.org. Harrisonhouse.com.

How Close Are We to the End?

Copyright © 2025 by Teaching You Can Trust, LLC
1814 W. Tacoma St.
Broken Arrow, OK 74012-1406

Published by Rick Renner Ministries
www.renner.org

ISBN 13: 978-1-6675-1497-0

ISBN 13 eBook: 978-1-6675-1498-7

All rights reserved. No portion of this book may be reproduced or transmitted in any form or by any means — electronic, mechanical, photocopy, recording, scanning, or other — except for brief quotations in critical reviews or articles, without the prior written permission of the Publisher.

7. "guide" — ὁδηγός (*hodegos*): a guide who shows a traveler the safest course through an unknown country; a guide who knows the safest, fastest, and most pleasurable route to take; a tour guide
8. "shew" — ἀναγγέλλω (*anangello*): to declare; to make clear; to clearly and vividly portray; to rehearse

SYNOPSIS

The ten lessons in this study titled ***How Close Are We to the End?*** will focus on the following topics:

- The Signs of His Coming
- End-Time Clarity for a Confused World
- Deception — The First Sign
- Wars, Rumors, and Your Peace
- Are Shortages a Sign of the End?
- Shockwaves and the Second Coming
- Deception. Wars. Earthquakes.
- False Prophets — What Did Jesus Say?
- End-Time Pressure vs. Your Faith
- When the Gospel Goes Global

We are living in unprecedented times. Yes, mankind has had problems since the beginning, but the challenges we see happening around the globe have put us in uncharted waters. Is the preponderance of bizarre and overwhelming events taking place today connected with biblical prophecy? If so, what do they tell us about where we are in time and how close we are to Christ's coming? Open your heart and your Bible as we explore what Jesus prophesied we would see before His return and the end of the age.

The emphasis of this lesson:

Matthew 24 captures a conversation between Jesus and His disciples in which He reveals more than 20 specific prophetic signs we will see before He comes and before the end of the age. This same conversation is also recorded in Mark 13 and Luke 21 and includes additional details.

What Jesus Said Came True

One day, as Jesus was leaving the Temple, He paused to teach His disciples something important. Matthew 24:1-2 says, "And Jesus went out, and departed from the temple: and his disciples came to him for to shew him the buildings of the temple. And Jesus said unto them, See ye not all these things? verily I say unto you, There shall not be left here one stone upon another, that shall not be thrown down."

Few things could have been more shocking to the disciples than these words from Jesus. The Temple was enormous. In fact, if you go to Jerusalem to see what is left of the retaining wall, you will see the huge stones; it's hard to imagine them being toppled down onto the ground. But Jesus told them a day was coming when the stones would fall and the Temple would no longer exist.

Although that seemed implausible to the disciples, that day came in 70 AD when Emperor Titus lay siege to the city of Jerusalem and destroyed the Temple. Today, when you visit the Holy City and walk along the bottom part of the retaining walls of the Temple, you'll see that the big stones were toppled from the Temple itself. They're lying there exactly as Jesus said, and they are a nearly 2,000-year-old prophetic declaration that everything else Jesus prophesied in Matthew 24 will also take place just as He said.

The Disciples Asked Jesus Questions About the End Times

After Jesus and the disciples made their way across the Kidron Valley and over to the Mount of Olives, they sat down and took in the panoramic view of the city of Jerusalem. Matthew 24:3 says, "And as he sat upon the mount of Olives, the disciples came unto him privately, saying, Tell us, when shall these things be? and what shall be the sign of thy coming, and of the end of the world?"

Notice that when the disciples were alone with Jesus, they felt the freedom to ask Him questions that He would not answer in front of the multitudes. This should encourage you to know that when you get alone with Jesus, He will answer your questions as well. In the disciples' case, they asked Jesus three specific questions:

1. When shall these things be?

2. What shall be the sign of thy coming?

3. What shall be the sign of the end of the world?

At that time in history, there was great interest in and fascination with end-time events. In addition to the people of Israel waiting for the coming of the Messiah — Jesus, who came without being recognized by the Jews — there was also a general obsession with and fixation on understanding *eschatology*, the study of end times. This was especially true during the 400 years between the Old and the New Testament. Thus, these three questions asked by the disciples were quite fitting.

Isn't it interesting that as we wait for Christ's return, once again, there is a fascination with and a fixation on end-time events? The Church has a sense that we're approaching the very end of things, and people are asking the same questions: "When shall these things be? What shall be the sign of thy coming and of the end of the age?"

Six Key Words in Matthew 24:3

Looking again at Matthew 24:3, we read, "And as he [Jesus] sat upon the mount of Olives, the disciples came unto him privately, saying, Tell us, when shall these things be? and what shall be the sign of thy coming, and of the end of the world?" In this passage, there are six very important words we need to understand. They are: "when," "what," "sign," "coming," "end," and "world." Let's unravel their meaning as we unpack the disciples' three questions.

'WHEN'

The first question the disciples asked Jesus was, "*When* shall these things be?" In Greek, the word "when" is the word *pote*, and it describes *specific information*. It signifies *one seeking a concrete answer*. Here, the disciples were questioning Jesus and asking, "*Exactly when* will the destruction of the Temple be, and when will all these things take place?" They felt the liberty to ask the Lord for very specific, concrete information, and so should you.

'WHAT'

The second question the disciples posed to Jesus was, "*What* shall be the sign of thy coming?" The word "what" here is the little Greek word *ti*, which describes *the most minute, minuscule detail*. The use of this word was the equivalent of the disciples asking Jesus, "*Exactly* and *explicitly* — down to the *minutest detail* — what will be the sign of Your coming." They didn't want general information. They wanted the very specific sign that would signify His coming.

'SIGN'

Jesus' most devoted followers asked Him for the "sign" of His coming. The word "sign" in Matthew 24:3 is the Greek word *semeion*, and it describes *a marker or sign to alert a traveler to where he is on a road*. This word denotes *authenticating marks* or *specific signs* that tell a person where he is.

Imagine you are in the former Soviet Union and planning to visit Rick and Denise Renner at their office, which is in the middle of Moscow. As you make your way toward their headquarters from the outlying areas, you will see beautiful pastures and forested land. As you continue down the road toward the city, there are signs to let you know the distance until you have reached your destination. As you travel, the surrounding environment changes. First, you will begin to see industries, followed by taller buildings, and finally more dense industry and even taller buildings.

Eventually, you'll cross a major highway called MKAD, and once you cross that road, you'll see a big sign that says *Moscow*. At that point, you're no longer traveling toward Moscow — you've *entered* it. All along the way, there are signs that tell you where you are on the road and how far you must go before you reach the city. If there were no signs, you would have no idea where you were on the road. But because of the signs and the changing environment, you are aware that you're heading somewhere significant — and you know how much farther you have to go before you get there.

What you just read depicts the meaning of the Greek word *semeion* — the word for "sign." The disciples' use of this word in Matthew 24:3 lets us know that as we journey from where we are to the end of the Church age, the environment is going to change. We're going to see alterations in culture, politics, government, and all throughout society. Jesus gave us a list in Matthew 24 of the changes we will see, and if we pay attention to the signs, we can determine where we are on the prophetic road as we head to the close of the age. He gave us these signs so that we can live informed and not ignorant about where we are in time.

Christ's 'COMING'

It is interesting to note that the disciples specifically wanted to know the sign of Jesus' "coming," which is the Greek word *parousia*. It is a technical expression for *the royal visit of a king or emperor* or *the arrival of one who alone has the authority to deal with the situation and put everything in correct order*. It is used interchangeably to describe both the rapture of the Church and the Second Coming of Christ, and the way to know how *parousia* is being used depends on the context of the surrounding verses.

Many claim that the word *parousia* only describes the Second Advent of Christ, which takes place at the very end of the seven-year Tribulation. Although it most certainly depicts Christ's Second Coming (the Second Advent), a survey of its use in the New Testament shows it also describes the coming of Christ at the time of the Rapture.

In Matthew 24:3, the disciples were asking the Lord, "Exactly when (*pote*) will these things be? Exactly and specifically what (*ti*) will be the authenticating sign (*semeion*) as we travel down this prophetic road to let us know Your coming (*parousia*) is here, and You are going to right every wrong and put everything in correct order?"

The 'END of the WORLD'

In addition to wanting to know when the Temple would be destroyed and when Jesus would return, the disciples also wanted to know the sign "…of the end of the world" (Matthew 24:3). In Greek, the word for "end" is *sunteleias*, which would better be translated *the closure, summation, or wrap-up of something*.

Equally important is the word "world," which is the Greek word *aionos*. Rather than describe the world, the earth, or the universe, the word *aionos* means *the age*. Therefore, a better translation of this portion of the verse would be, "How will we know that we're approaching the closure or the wrap up of the age?" That is what the disciples were asking Jesus, and that's the focus of this entire series.

These same questions and concerns of Jesus' disciples then are also what are on the minds of many people today. Maybe you've been asking these questions. If so, Jesus wants you to be at peace. He has everything under control. Although the present age we are in is going to come to an end and this world will be refined by fire, the world itself is never going to end.

Jesus Provided a Detailed List of Signs

As the disciples were alone with Jesus, they asked Him for the *one* sign that would mark His coming (*see* Matthew 24:3). But instead of giving them just one sign, Jesus provided 22 specific signs that we would see on our journey toward the wrap-up or consummation of all things. These signs are listed in three of the four gospels: Matthew 24:4-14; Mark 13:5-13; Luke 21:8-19.

1. **Worldwide deception** (Matthew 24:4; Mark 13:5; Luke 21:8)
2. **Deception in the Church** (Matthew 24:5; Mark 13:6; Luke 21:8)
3. **Wars** (Matthew 24:6; Mark 13:7; Luke 21:9)
4. **Rumors of wars** (Matthew 24:6; Mark 13:7)
5. **Commotions** (Luke 21:9)
6. **Widespread terrorism** (Luke 21:9)
7. **Warring political systems** (Matthew 24:7; Mark 13:8; Luke 21:10)
8. **Clash of culture** (Matthew 24:7; Mark 13:8; Luke 21:10)
9. **Ethnic conflicts** (Matthew 24:7; Mark 13:8; Luke 21:10)
10. **Famines** (Matthew 24:7; Mark 13:8; Luke 21:11)
11. **Economic instability** (Matthew 24:7; Mark 13:8; Luke 21:11)
12. **Pestilences** (Matthew 24:7; Luke 21:11)
13. **Unknown diseases** (Matthew 24:7; Luke 21:11)
14. **Great seismic activity** (Matthew 24:7; Mark 13:8; Luke 21:11)
15. **Widespread persecution of believers** (Matthew 24:9; Mark 13:9; Luke 21:12)
16. **Legal prosecution of Christians** (Matthew 24:9; Mark 13:9,11; Luke 21:12)
17. **Imprisonment of believers** (Matthew 24:9; Mark 13:9,11; Luke 21:12)
18. **Emergence of false prophets** (Matthew 24:11)
19. **Love of many waxing cold** (Matthew 24:12)
20. **Fearful sights** (Luke 21:11)
21. **Signs from the heavens** (Luke 21:11)
22. **Worldwide preaching of the Gospel** (Matthew 24:14; Mark 13:10)

Jesus named all these specific signs we would see before His return and before the end of the age. In reality, we have seen many of these signs taking place for years — in some cases, thousands of years. However, Jesus said that as we come to the "end of the world" — the *closure* or *wrap up* (*sunteleias*) of the *age* (*aionos*) — these signs will increase in number, in frequency, and in intensity.

The Holy Spirit Is Our 'Guide' for the End Times

Jesus went on to say, "But of that day and hour knoweth no man, no, not the angels of heaven, but my Father only" (Matthew 24:36). These words from Jesus put us on notice that we're wasting our time when we set dates as to when the rapture of the Church is going to take place. When people do this, it causes others to doubt the reality of the Rapture and even the truth of the Bible itself. If Jesus does not know the day and hour of His coming and the angels of Heaven don't know either, then who are we to think we can find the date?

To be clear, that doesn't mean we can't know the season. In Matthew 24:33, Jesus said, "…When ye shall see all these things, know that it is near, even at the doors." So, if we will listen to the Holy Spirit, He will alert us to where we are in time.

As a matter of fact, in John 16:13, Jesus revealed that a major role of the Holy Spirit is a prophetic role:

> **Howbeit when he, the Spirit of truth, is come, he will guide you into all truth: for he shall not speak of himself; but whatsoever he shall hear, that shall he speak: and he will shew you things to come.**

The word "guide" in this verse is the Greek word *hodegos*. It is taken from the word *hodas*, which is the Greek word for *a road*. But when this word *hodas* becomes *hodegos*, it describes a person who is *a tour guide* or *a road guide*. By using this word, Jesus is saying the Holy Spirit wants to be your tour guide.

Just like you might hire a professional guide to take you on an excursion or a tour, you have the Holy Spirit in you to help you navigate through life — and He knows all the roads! He sees everything in front of you and knows everything that's going to happen eschatologically in the future. If you'll allow Him, He'll show you where to go and where not to go. He'll alert you as to what's going to happen next and show you how to prepare for it.

Jesus said that the Holy Spirit will "...speak: and he will shew you things to come" (John 16:13). And the word "shew" is the Greek word, *anangello*, which means *to declare; to make clear; to clearly, vividly portray;* or even *to rehearse*. The first part of the word, *ana*, means *to do it again and again*, which indicates that if we will listen to the Holy Spirit and allow Him to be our *Tour Guide*, He'll show us where to go and declare to us over and over again "things to come" (John 16:13).

The original Greek text in John 16:13, translated as the phrase "things to come," would be better translated as *the things that are coming*. Even though we cannot pinpoint a date of Christ's coming, if we will listen to the Holy Spirit and allow him to be our Guide (*hodegas*), He will quicken to us what's happening around us. Instead of just seeing what is happening in the news, if we'll listen to the Spirit of God, He'll reveal to us what's happening behind the scenes in the unseen realm of the spirit and how all the events fit together as we come to the wrap up of this current age.

In our next lesson, we will take a closer look at where we are in time in light of our current events and all the signs Jesus prophesied would take place.

STUDY QUESTIONS

Study to shew thyself approved unto God, a workman that needeth not to be ashamed, rightly dividing the word of truth.
— 2 Timothy 2:15

1. When it comes to Jesus' soon return, what do the Scriptures say about what we can and can't know? And what did Jesus say to look for?
   - Matthew 24:36, 25:13; and Mark 13:32
   - Matthew 24:32-34; Mark 13:28-30; and Luke 21:28-32

2. The Holy Spirit is your *Tour Guide* who knows all the roads! He sees everything in front of you and knows everything that's going to happen in the future. What specific, concrete wisdom or direction do you need right now? Take a few moments to pray and ask the Holy Spirit to reveal to you what you need to know to make the best decisions for you and your family. (Consider and stand on God's promises to you in Psalm 32:8; John 16:13; and James 1:5.)

PRACTICAL APPLICATION

> But be ye doers of the word, and not hearers only,
> deceiving your own selves.
> —James 1:22

1. No doubt, we are living in unprecedented times. There are things taking place around us so fast and so frequently that it is difficult to keep up with everything. From your perspective, what are some of the most bizarre things you see taking place in the world and in your own region?
2. In Matthew 24, Jesus gives us more than 20 specific signs regarding His coming to rapture the Church and the end of the age (*see* the detailed list in this lesson). How many of these end-time markers can you actually see happening right now near you and around the world?

LESSON 2

TOPIC
End-Time Clarity for a Confused World

SCRIPTURES
1. **Matthew 24:3** — And as he sat upon the mount of Olives, the disciples came unto him privately, saying, Tell us, when shall these things be? and what shall be the sign of thy coming, and of the end of the world?
2. **Matthew 24:4** — And Jesus answered and said unto them, Take heed that no man deceive you.

GREEK WORDS
1. "when" — **ποτέ** (*pote*): exactly when; indicates specific information
2. "what" — **τι** (*ti*): minute, minuscule detail; exactly; explicitly
3. "sign" — **σημεῖον** (*semeion*): a marker or sign used to alert a traveler to where he is on a road; authenticating marks or specific signs

4. "coming" — **παρουσία** (*parousia*): to be present; a technical expression for the royal visit of a king or emperor; the arrival of one who alone has the authority to deal with a situation and put things in correct order
5. "end" — **συντέλειας** (*sunteleias*): the closure, the summation, or wrap-up of the age
6. "world" — **αἰῶνος** (*aionos*): not the world itself, but the age
7. "last" — **ἔσχατος** (*eschatos*): the ultimate end of a thing; the extreme end; used in classical Greek literature to depict the place furthest away, such as the very end of the earth; the final port or last stopping off point of a journey; something that is final; the very end

SYNOPSIS

Have you ever wondered when Jesus was coming again? Or what would be the signs we would see just prior to His return? If so, you're not alone. Many believers are asking those same questions. In fact, the disciples of Christ were searching for answers to those very questions all the way back in the First Century. In this lesson, we will unpack Christ's candid conversation with His disciples and learn about the birth pains Jesus prophesied we would experience during these last of the last days.

The emphasis of this lesson:

We are in the last of the last days. We have sailed almost to the end of the age of grace, and we are experiencing "birth pains" just as Jesus said. The next major event on the prophetic calendar is the rapture of the Church, which will trigger the seven-year Tribulation.

The Disciples' Candid Conversation With Christ

Toward the end of Jesus' earthly ministry, He made a statement to the disciples regarding the impending destruction of the Temple. He declared, "…See ye not all these things? verily I say unto you, There shall not be left here one stone upon another, that shall not be thrown down" (Matthew 24:2).

Greatly perplexed by Jesus' words, the disciples waited for an opportunity when they were alone with Him and away from the multitudes to ask Him what He meant. The Bible says, "And as he sat upon the mount of Olives, the disciples came unto him privately, saying, Tell us, when shall these things be? and what shall be the sign of thy coming, and of the end of the world?" (Matthew 24:3)

We saw in Lesson 1 that in the First Century, as well as during the intertestamental period between the Old and New Testaments, there was a fixation on *eschatology*, which is *the study of end-time events*. People were very preoccupied with discovering the prophetic signs connected with the end of the age. It became an obsession with God's people, which is what we have seen resurface in our present day. The reason this is happening is we're coming close to the rapture of the Church. Just as there was a fixation on end-time events before Christ's first coming, there's a renewed interest in end-time events as we approach the Rapture and the Second Coming of Christ.

Again, the disciples asked, "…When shall these things be? and what shall be the sign of thy coming, and of the end of the world?" (Matthew 24:3). We learned that there are several important words in this passage that are included in these questions the disciples asked.

'*When* shall these things be?'

The disciples' first question starts with the word "when," the Greek word *pote*. It describes *specific information*. The disciples were asking Jesus to reveal *exactly when* the Temple would be destroyed, as well as *precisely when* He was coming back and *exactly when* the end of the world would be. They felt the liberty to ask the Lord for very specific, concrete information, and so should you.

'*What* shall be the sign of thy coming?'

This second question begins with the word "what," which is a translation of the little Greek word *ti*. It describes *the most minute, miniscule detail*. The use of this word lets us know that the disciples were saying, "Lord, don't be vague or leave us in the dark. Please tell us *exactly and explicitly* what the sign of Your coming will be."

The disciples asked for a '*sign*.'

The Greek word for "sign" in Matthew 24:3 is the word *semeion*, and it describes *a marker or sign to alert a traveler to where he is on a road*. This *authenticating mark or sign* also tells a person how much farther he must travel before he reaches his destination.

In Lesson 1, Rick gave an example of traveling to the RENNER Ministries office in Moscow. As you journey from their home, which is about seven and a half miles outside the city limits, you will see the signs change along the road, and the environment itself will begin to change as you make your way toward the city. First you will encounter pastures and beautiful trees. That will give way to an industry sector followed by tall apartment buildings and then multitudes of apartment complexes. The closer you get to Moscow, the more congested the surroundings become. Finally, when you reach MKAD Highway, which is the big beltway that encircles the city, there is a huge sign that says *Moscow*. It is the sign indicating you're no longer traveling *toward* Moscow — you've *entered* it.

This illustrates the Greek word *semeion*, which is translated in Matthew 24:3 as the word "sign." Interestingly, this word *semeion* was also used to describe literal *road signs* or *road markers* that tell a person where he or she is and how far he or she must go before reaching the destination. Every few kilometers or miles there's a new sign with a different number.

By using this word "sign," the Greek word *semeion*, the disciples were literally asking the Lord, "What is the prophetic sign we will see on the road to the end of the age that will confirm to us that we are at the end and You are about to come?" Although the disciples only asked for one sign, Jesus gave 22 signs. That's what happens when you get alone with the Lord. When you ask Him a question, He will answer, and if your ears are open, He'll tell you many other things as well (*see* Jeremiah 33:3).

Christ's 'Coming' and the 'End of the World'

The disciples asked specifically for the sign of Jesus' *coming*, and the word "coming" here is the Greek word *parousia*. Theologically, the word *parousia* is used to describe both the rapture of the Church and the Second Advent, which will take place seven years later at the end of the Tribulation. Some people argue that this word *parousia* only describes the Second Advent, but that's not true. A careful study of the New Testament reveals that this word is used to describe both events. To determine which event it is referring to depends on the context of the surrounding verses.

Most importantly, this word *parousia* is *a technical expression for the royal visit of a king or an emperor or for the arrival of one who alone has the authority and power to deal with the situation and put things in correct order, making everything right.* Friend, when Jesus comes to rapture the Church, that's the moment He will begin putting things in order. The Rapture will trigger and initiate the seven-year Tribulation, which will begin the release of God's wrath upon the earth as He deals with His enemies.

At the end of the Tribulation, Jesus is going to return with us, which will be the culmination of the *parousia*. In that Second Advent, we're going to put our feet on the ground with Jesus, and it will begin His millennial reign.

In addition to the sign of Christ's coming, the disciples also wanted to know the sign for "the end of the world" (Matthew 24:3). We saw that the word "world" here is *aionos*, which is not the earth itself, but *the age*, and the word "end" is the Greek word *sunteleias*, which describes *the closure* or *the summation of the age*. Rather than describe the ultimate end, it refers to *the wrap up*.

The disciples' question in Matthew 24:3 was essentially, "Lord, *exactly when* (*pote*) are these things going to happen? Tell us *exactly what* (*ti*), down to *the smallest factual detail*, the *major road sign* (*semeion*) we'll see along the prophetic road to alert us that we're very near to Your coming (*parousia*), when You're going to return and begin the process of dealing with the situation and putting everything in correct order. And tell us how we will know we've come to *the consummation, the closure*, or to *the wrap up of the age*?"

That is what the disciples were asking and were fixated on in the First Century, and it is what God's people are still asking today.

We're in the 'Last Days'

Imagine you are drawing a timeline of prophetic events. On the extreme left would be our starting point, which would be Jesus' death on the Cross and His resurrection from the grave. That took place in the year 33 AD.

Then 50 days later was the Day of Pentecost. According to Acts 2, Pentecost happened in 33 AD at 9:00 a.m. After the Holy Spirit was poured out on the disciples gathered in the upper room, Peter stood up and spoke to the crowd of onlookers who were perplexed by what they were hearing. He said, "For these are not drunken, as ye suppose, seeing it is but the third hour of the day [9:00 a.m.]" (Acts 2:15). Peter then declared:

> **But this is that which was spoken by the prophet Joel; And it shall come to pass in the last days, saith God, I will pour out of my Spirit upon all flesh....**
>
> — Acts 2:16-17

In this passage, Peter was quoting Joel 2:28, where God said, "And it shall come to pass afterward, that I will pour out my spirit upon all flesh...." The Bible documents the exact timing of the outpouring of the Holy Spirit — 9:00 a.m. in the year 33 AD. Thus, the outpouring of the Spirit began at that time and has lasted for nearly 2,000 years.

This period in which we live is officially called *the last days*. To this day, the Holy Spirit continues to be poured out and will continue His outpouring all the way to the end of these last days. Some people call this *the Church age*, which is very appropriate because the Church was birthed at its beginning, and it will continue until Christ comes to rapture the Church at the end of the age.

This same era is also called by some people as *the age of grace*, which is also true because it is the period in which God's grace has been poured out on mankind. When we reach the end of this age, the world is going to experience a rude awakening and discover that the age of God's grace has ended. Nevertheless, for the last 2,000 years we've been living in the age of grace, or the Church age. In biblical terms, these are *the last days* — a 2,000-year era that is soon coming to an end.

The Last-Days World Will Experience 'Birth Pains'

It is interesting to note that the Greek word for "last," as in the last days, is *eschatos*. It describes *the ultimate end of a thing* or *the extreme end*, and it is where we get the word *eschatology*. This word was used in classical Greek literature to depict *the place furthest away*, such as *the very end of the earth*. The Greek word *eschatos* was also a navigational term used to denote *the final port or last stopping off point of a journey*. Once a person sailed to the *eschatos*, there was not another port to sail to after that. This was *something final — the very end*.

This word *eschatos* is the very word the Holy Spirit prompted Paul to use to describe the very end of the Church age, the very last of the last days. That is where we are right now. We have sailed to the very end of the age of grace, and Jesus said when we reach that point, the world is going to experience "birth pains." The *King James Version* translates this as "sorrows" in Matthew 24:8. It is the Greek word *oodin*, and it describes *the pain necessary to open up or to introduce something new.*

Rick shared how when his wife, Denise, was pregnant with their first son, she came to a point in her pregnancy when she began experiencing birth pains — also known as *contractions*. Initially, the birth pains were mild and far apart. But as time passed and she drew closer to delivery, the contractions got closer, came faster, and were increasingly intense. These were the signs that their son Paul was about to be born.

In the same way, as we come to the end of the age, it is going to culminate with intensifying birth pains. Interestingly, if you study Scripture, every age ends with pains that give birth to the next age. And these birth pains usually come in the form of worldwide events that are tragic. The closer we get to the end of the age, the faster, more intense, and more frequently these things are going to happen.

Without question, we are living at a time when we're experiencing tumultuous events, one on top of the next. Fifty years ago, if one of these things happened, it was big news. But now that these things are happening so fast, so frequently, and so furiously, the world is nearly numb to the chaotic state of things — such events are now treated as normal. We're living in the middle of tragedy all the time.

Remember, the apostles asked the Lord, "How will we know when we've come to the end of this particular age?" Jesus answered and basically said, "You will know you've come to the last of the last days (*eschatos*) because the earth will be experiencing birth pains (*oodin*) at the very end of the age."

The Church Is About To Be Raptured

At the very, very end of the age — as the closure, the summation, or wrap up takes place — Jesus is going to suddenly come for the Church. The dead in Christ will be raised to new life, and the spiritually vibrant believers who are living on the earth will be caught up to meet them and the Lord in the air (*see* 1 Thessalonians 4:17). This is the rapture of the Church.

For a period of seven years, believers will be in Heaven enjoying a glorious time of reunion and celebration. During those seven years, the marriage feast of the Lamb will take place, when Christ and the Church will finally be joined together as one (*see* Revelation 19:7-9). Also, during these seven years, every believer will be brought before the judgment (or *bema*) seat of Christ (*see* 2 Corinthians 5:10). One by one, we're going to be summoned from our place at the table to stand before Jesus, and He is going to evaluate the works we did on the earth to determine what we're going to be doing in eternity.

Make no mistake: Eternity is going to be very active. We're not just going to be sitting around on clouds playing harps. We are each going to be given divine assignments, and our time here on the earth is prequalification for those future assignments.

While we are in Heaven, God's wrath is going to be poured out upon the earth. The Bible calls this the Tribulation. As believers, we will not be here during that time. According to Scripture, at the conclusion of those seven years, Jesus will return to the earth. Unlike the Rapture, which will take place in secret and in the air, Christ's Second Coming will be public, and He'll step down on the Mount of Olives with all His saints. That's us! All of us who will have been in Heaven will return with Jesus at the end of the Tribulation, and He will crush evil at that moment and begin His millennial reign from Jerusalem.

The Number-One Indicator

So what is the most glaring sign Jesus gave the disciples — which includes us — that will mark the last days? What is the number one, foremost sign He provided to indicate that the end of the age and His coming were upon us? The answer is in Matthew 24:4. In this verse, "…Jesus answered and said unto them, Take heed that no man deceive you." Hence, *worldwide deception* is the most blatant sign that we have come to the very end of the age, and this sign is so important, we are going to take all of our next lesson to unpack it.

STUDY QUESTIONS

> **Study to shew thyself approved unto God, a workman that needeth not to be ashamed, rightly dividing the word of truth.**
> **— 2 Timothy 2:15**

1. Jesus' coming to rapture the Church is alluded to and talked about in other New Testament passages. To help you understand this profound event that is next on God's prophetic calendar, take time to look up these verses and write the details they give about Christ's return.
   - How close are we to His coming? (*See* Hebrews 10:37; James 5:7-8; Revelation 3:11.)
   - Jesus said His coming will be like what other time in Bible history? (*See* Matthew 24:36-41; Luke 17:26-36.)
   - How does the Bible describe Jesus' coming? (*See* 1 Thessalonians 5:1-4; 2 Peter 3:10; Revelation 3:3; 16:15.)
2. To make sure we don't miss Jesus' coming to rapture us, what did He repeatedly instruct us to do in Matthew 24:42-44; 25:13; Mark 13:32-37; Luke 12:35-40; and 21:34-36? Are you heeding His warning?

PRACTICAL APPLICATION

> But be ye doers of the word, and not hearers only, deceiving your own selves.
> —James 1:22

1. What new insights are you learning about *the last days* and *the age of grace*? What about the *birth pains* Jesus said we would experience and the timing of His coming to rapture us, His Church? What are you seeing and understanding that you didn't understand before?
2. Jesus compared the signs that will precede His coming and the end of the age with *birth pains* or *contractions* a woman in labor experiences before having her baby. How does this imagery help you better understand the difficult events we can expect to take place in these last of the last days?

LESSON 3

TOPIC
Deception — The First Sign

SCRIPTURES
1. **Matthew 24:3** — And as he sat upon the mount of Olives, the disciples came unto him privately, saying, Tell us, when shall these things be? and what shall be the sign of thy coming, and of the end of the world?
2. **Matthew 24:4** — And Jesus answered and said unto them, Take heed that no man deceive you.
3. **2 Thessalonians 2:3** — Let no man deceive you by any means: for that day shall not come, except there come a falling away first, and that man of sin be revealed, the son of perdition.
4. **2 Thessalonians 2:11** — And for this cause God shall send them strong delusion, that they should believe a lie.
5. **Romans 1:28** — And even as they did not like to retain God in their knowledge, God gave them over to a reprobate mind, to do those things which are not convenient.

GREEK WORDS
1. "take heed" — βλέπω (*blepo*): watch; listen; pay attention; intended to jar and jolt his listeners
2. "deceive" — πλανάω (*planao*): pictures deception or a moral wandering; depicts a person (or nation) who has veered from a solid path as a result of wandering morally; also used to depict a lost animal that can't find its way; to morally lose one's bearings; to wander off course
3. "falling away" — ἀποστασία (*apostasia*): a compound of ἀπό (*apo*) and ἵστημι (*histimi*); ἀπό (*apo*) means away, and ἵστημι (*histimi*) means to stand; compounded, they form a word that means to stand apart from; to distance one's self from; to step away from, to withdraw from, or to shrink away from; it is from this very Greek word that we derive the word apostate or apostasy; a falling away or revolt; describes political revolt; a mutiny
4. "first" — πρῶτον (*proton*): first in order; in first place; to begin with

5. "revealed"— ἀποκάλυψις (*apokalupsis*): to uncover, reveal, or unveil; to pull the curtains apart
6. "for this cause"— καὶ διὰ τοῦτο (*kai dia touto*): for this reason; because of this; pictures God's response to their choice
7. "strong delusion"— ἐνέργειαν πλάνης (*energeian planes*): from the words ἐνεργέω (*energeo*) and πλανάω (*planao*); the word ἐνεργέω (*energeo*) is where we get the word energy and depicts a force propelling something forward or an energy that ignites a process and facilitates it all the way to its conclusion; the word πλανάω (*planao*) pictures wandering or deviant behavior; together, they describe an energized wandering

SYNOPSIS

Did you know that Jesus gave us one *major* sign to alert us that His coming and the end of the age were near? He mentioned this sign four times in Matthew 24; three times in Mark 13; and once in Luke 21. What is this mega-sign Jesus alluded to a total of eight times in these three gospels? It is *deception*.

The emphasis of this lesson:

The primary sign Jesus gave to indicate we are nearing the end of the age is worldwide deception. Jesus prophesied that at the very end of the age, society worldwide is going to go so far off track morally that they will lose their way and be unable to return to the moral path where they used to be.

The Disciples Had Questions Just Like We Do

One day, as Jesus' disciples were marveling at the immensity and beauty of the Temple, He turned to them and said, "…See ye not all these things? verily I say unto you, There shall not be left here one stone upon another, that shall not be thrown down" (Matthew 24:2). No doubt, these words were shocking and quite overwhelming for the disciples, which motivated them to seek clarification.

Matthew 24:3 says, "And as he [Jesus] sat upon the mount of Olives, the disciples came unto him privately, saying, Tell us, when shall these things be? and what shall be the sign of thy coming, and of the end of the world?"

These questions reveal how the disciples were obsessed with knowing prophetic issues. In fact, the world of the First Century in Israel was very fixated on the end of the age.

Today, we are living in the last of the last days, and people are once again preoccupied and even obsessed with a deep interest in prophetic events or things of an eschatological nature. Many can sense that something significant is about to happen — the same kind of things they were sensing at Jesus' first coming.

What is interesting is that the disciples only asked for *one* single sign, but when Jesus answered them, He gave them more than 20 signs, which are recorded in Matthew 24, Mark 13, and Luke 21. Most people would say that the foremost sign that we've come to the end of the age is the restoration of Israel as a nation. Although that certainly is a major sign, it is not the overarching sign Jesus gave to indicate that we've sailed to the very end of the age.

The First Sign Jesus Gave Is Worldwide Deception

In Matthew 24:4, we find the number one sign that Jesus repeatedly talked about that confirms we are in the last of the last days. Here, the Bible says, "And Jesus answered and said unto them, Take heed that no man deceive you." Hence, *worldwide deception* will be rampant at the end of the age.

In this verse, there are two key words you need to understand. First is the phrase "take heed." It is a form of the Greek word *blepo*, which means *watch*, *listen*, or *pay attention*. It is spoken in a strong tense and is intended to jar and jolt the listeners. It is as if Jesus was saying, "Stand up, throw your shoulders back, open your ears, watch, listen, be attentive, and really pay attention."

Once Jesus had obtained the disciples' full focus, He unveiled the first and foremost sign that will mark the end of the age saying, "…Take heed that no man deceive you" (Mathew 24:4). The word "deceive" here is a form of the Greek word *planao*, which depicts *a deceptive, moral wandering*. It was a word used frequently by rabbis and spiritual leaders during the intertestamental period to prophetically forecast what was going to happen in society at the very end of the age.

This word *planao* — translated here as "deceive" — describes *a moral wandering* and depicts *a people who have veered from a solid path and now teeter on a dangerously treacherous moral route*. As Jesus warned against deception, He was alerting us to the fact that in the last days, demonic spirits will cause society to leave a well-trodden, safe, traditional path and will cause people to go in a new direction. They will gradually throw away all the morals of the past and replace them with new ideas, perhaps even calling them "progressive" ideas.

What is also very important about this word *planao* is that it was used in an agricultural sense to describe an animal that had wandered away and had become so lost it couldn't find its way back home. Thus, we're not talking about a little veering or a little wandering. We're talking about major deviation. By using this word *planao* (deceive), Jesus prophesied that at the very end of the age, society worldwide is going to go so far off track morally that they will lose their way and be unable to return to the moral path where they used to be.

This worldwide moral wandering Jesus forecasted would take place at the end of the age is exactly what we are witnessing with our own eyes today. Not only are we seeing individuals wandering off course, but also whole nations that are veering away from a moral position they once held to be true.

Deception Will Manifest as Apostasy in the Church

The deception that Jesus warned about in Matthew 24:4 is connected to what the apostle Paul wrote about in Second Thessalonians 2. To grasp the connection, you need to first understand that the Thessalonian believers were very upset because someone they trusted had told them that the rapture of the Church had already happened. That meant the day of the Lord had begun, and the Thessalonian believers were living in the Tribulation. Of course, that wasn't true, which is why Paul took time to write them a second letter.

In Second Thessalonians 2:3, Paul said, "Let no man deceive you by any means: for that day shall not come, except there come a falling away first, and that man of sin be revealed, the son of perdition." The words "that day" refer to the rapture of the Church and the start of the Tribulation. Paul informed these precious new believers that the Rapture (and the initiation of the Tribulation) could not begin "…except there come a falling away first…" (2 Thessalonians 2:3).

The words "falling away" are a translation of the Greek word *apostasia*, a compound of the words *apo* and *histimi*. The word *apo* means *away* and carries the idea of *putting distance between you and something else*, and the word *histimi* means *to stand*. When compounded, they form the word *apostasia*, which means *to stand apart from* and implies the distancing of one's self from something one used to be close to. It means *to step away from, to withdraw from,* or *to shrink away from*. It is from this very Greek word that we derive the words *apostate* and *apostasy*, which is a picture of a person or groups of people who once were very close to the faith, even walking in faith, but now — *apostasia* — they've stepped away from what they used to believe.

Being a linguist, Paul was familiar with the meaning of the word *apostasia* as it was commonly used throughout Greek literature. Under the guidance of the Holy Spirit, he chose this word purposely to communicate what would be happening in the Church just before the return of Christ.

The 'Falling Away' Is a Mutinous Revolt Against God

Some people today try to infer that the word *apostasia* used in Second Thessalonians 2:3 is another way of describing the Rapture, but that is incorrect. Historically, the word *apostasia* describes *a falling away* or *a revolt* and was often used to denote *a political revolt, a mutiny,* or *a mutinous attitude*. Every single time this word is used, that's what it means, and that's what it means here. Therefore, in this verse, the apostle Paul was saying, "At the very end of the age, before the Rapture and before the Tribulation begins, there is going to emerge a worldwide spiritual mutiny against the rule of God and the Word of God." This fits very well with the word "deceive," the Greek word *planao*, which describes *a worldwide moral wandering* that causes society to get completely off track.

Paul said this global mutiny against the law of God is going to happen "first." In Greek, the word "first" is the word *proton*, which means *first in order, in first place,* or *to begin with*. Hence, before the Rapture happens and before the day of the Lord begins, a worldwide mutiny is going to happen first.

Then Paul said, "…And that man of sin be revealed, the son of perdition" (2 Thessalonians 2:3). The one who will be revealed is none other than the Antichrist. Paul calls him the "man of sin," which literally means the "Lawless One.' He is also called the "Son of Perdition," which indicates that everything he touches will turn to rot and ruin.

Paul said that at the appointed time, the Antichrist will be "revealed," which is the Greek word *apokalupsis* and means *to uncover, reveal, unveil*, or *to pull the curtains apart*. The use of this word here lets us know that the Antichrist is going to be center stage but veiled, waiting for his big debut. He can't be revealed until the world is first primed and prepared to receive him.

Think about it — if the Antichrist had appeared 50 years ago, the world would have never received him because 50 years ago, many people were still established in Judeo-Christian principles. Today things are different. For decades, the world has been morally wandering from the time-tested path of Judeo-Christian principles. Many of the younger generation don't even know what those principles are. They have become lawless in their beliefs, and in a great sense, the new "woke" environment of the world is a mutinous rebellion against the law of God. Clearly, the world at large is deceived and has a mutinous rebellious attitude toward the instructions and the law of God. All of that has to happen first — *before* the rapture of the Church and the day of the Lord takes place.

When we factor in the original Greek meaning of the key words in this verse, the *Renner Interpretive Version* (*RIV*) of 2 Thessalonians 2:3 says:

> **In light of these things, I urge you to refuse to allow anyone to take advantage of you in any way. For example, you won't need a letter to tell you when the day of the Lord has come; you ought to know by now — that day can't come until first a worldwide insurgency, rebellion, riot, and mutiny against God has come about in society. Once that occurs, the world will be primed, prepared, and ready to embrace the man of lawlessness — the one who hates law and has rebellion running in his blood. This is the long-awaited and predicted son of doom and destruction, the one who brings rot and ruin to everything he touches. When the time is just right, he will finally come out of hiding and go public.**

Those Who Reject God Will Get What They Want

Second Thessalonians 2:11 says, "And for this cause God shall send them strong delusion, that they should believe a lie." Essentially, because the world at large will reject the will of God and reject His Word, God will give them what they want. Similarly, in Romans 1:28, the apostle Paul said, "And even as they did not like to retain God in their knowledge, God gave them over to a reprobate mind, to do those things which are not convenient."

Some read this verse and think it's a picture of God just washing His hands of people, but that is not what it means. A better interpretation would be, "And for this cause, God released them...." The phrase "for this cause" is a translation of the Greek words *kai dia touto*, which means *for this reason* or *because of this*. It pictures God's response to the people's choice.

What is *strong delusion*? It is an English translation derived from two Greek words. The first is the word *energeo*, which is from where we get the word *energy*, and it depicts *a force propelling something forward* or *an energy that ignites a process and facilitates it all the way to its conclusion*. The second word is *planao*, which we have already seen, and it pictures *wandering or deviant behavior*. When these words are compounded, they form the Greek word *energeian planes*, which describes *an energized wandering*. The use of this word here tells us that what people want, God will release them to have.

When we factor in the original Greek meaning of the key words in this verse, the *Renner Interpretive Version* (*RIV*) of 2 Thessalonians 2:11 says:

God will give them what they want and send delusion and error into their midst, compelling them to believe the lie that is being offered to them.

When we take the meaning in this verse and what Jesus said in Matthew 24:4, we see that at the very end of the age, worldwide deception will be an epidemic. It is the number one sign Jesus gave to indicate that we are in the last days, which is why He urged us, "…Take heed that no man deceive you" (Matthew 24:4). He's saying, "Stand up, throw your shoulders back, open your ears, watch, listen, and really pay attention.

A worldwide moral wandering is going to take place at the time of the end — don't be swept away in it!"

In our next lesson, we will look at the signs of wars and rumors of wars, commotions, and what Jesus meant by nation rising against nation and kingdom rising against kingdom at the end of the age.

STUDY QUESTIONS

> Study to shew thyself approved unto God, a workman that needeth not to be ashamed, rightly dividing the word of truth.
> — 2 Timothy 2:15

1. How has culture changed since the time you were growing up? In what ways have you personally witnessed society become deceived and morally wander away from the moral path of truth it once walked?
2. What is the number-one way to guard against being deceived in these last days? It is *feeding your soul and spirit the unchanging truth of God's Word!* To help you understand some of the life-giving benefits of reading, studying, and meditating on Scripture, check out these powerful promises:
   - The Word *gives life*: Psalm 19:7-11; Proverbs 4:20-22; Jeremiah 15:16; 1 Peter 2:2
   - The Word *purifies*: Psalm 119:9,11; John 15:3; 17:17; 1 Peter 1:22
   - The Word *teaches and equips*: Acts 20:32; Romans 15:4; 2 Timothy 3:16-17
   - The Word *transforms*: Romans 1:16; Hebrews 4:12; James 1:21-25

PRACTICAL APPLICATION

> But be ye doers of the word, and not hearers only, deceiving your own selves.
> — James 1:22

1. A "deceived" person is someone who once walked on a solid path of truth but has drifted and is now teetering on the edge of a treacherous moral route. In many ways, this person is just like an animal that has wandered away and has become so lost it can't find its way back home. In view of this definition, are there any places in your life where

deception has crept in and taken you captive? Are there areas in which you've drifted from the solid, biblical belief you once had? If so, what are they?
2. In what ways have you deviated from the previous, time-tested biblical standards and moral positions you once held to? What were you once doing that you are no longer doing?
3. If God is revealing something to you, welcome the conviction of His Holy Spirit. It is because He loves you that He is pointing out the error of your ways and drawing you back to Himself. Repent of any sin and ask Him for His grace to get back on the path of truth.

LESSON 4

TOPIC

Wars, Rumors, and Your Peace

SCRIPTURES

1. **Matthew 24:3** — And as he sat upon the mount of Olives, the disciples came unto him privately, saying, Tell us, when shall these things be? and what shall be the sign of thy coming, and of the end of the world?
2. **Matthew 24:4** — And Jesus answered and said unto them, Take heed that no man deceive you.
3. **Matthew 24:6** — And ye shall hear of wars and rumours of wars: see that ye be not troubled: for all these things must come to pass, but the end is not yet.
4. **Luke 21:9** — But when ye shall hear of wars and commotions, be not terrified: for these things must first come to pass; but the end is not by and by.
5. **Matthew 24:7** — For nation shall rise against nation, and kingdom against kingdom….

GREEK WORDS

1. "take heed" — βλέπω (*blepo*): watch; listen; pay attention; intended to jar and jolt his listeners

2. "deceive" — **πλανάω** (*planao*): pictures deception or a moral wandering; depicts a person (or nation) who has veered from a solid path as a result of wandering morally; also used to depict a lost animal that can't find its way; to morally lose one's bearings; to wander off course
3. "hear" — **ἀκούω** (*akouo*): to hear; acoustics
4. "wars" — **πόλεμος** (*polemos*): describes armed conflicts, plural, which would include battles, fights, skirmishes, and large-scale conflicts
5. "rumors" — **ἀκοή** (*akoe*): ear; something heard in the ear; hence, rumor
6. "troubled" — **θροέω** (*throeo*): inward fright that causes one to be filled with worry, anxiety, or fear; worry and inward anxiety resulting from outward events that keep occurring repeatedly
7. "end" — **τέλος** (*telos*): the ultimate conclusion or climax of a thing
8. "commotions" — **ἀκαταστασία** (*akatastasia*): instability; out of control; upheaval; anarchy; turbulent upheavals of a societal, political, or militaristic nature
9. "terrified" — **πτοέω** (*ptoeo*): an inward fluttering; panic or terror; to be terrorized; a fright that results from something that startles or alarms; pictures terrorism
10. "end" — **τέλος** (*telos*): the ultimate conclusion or climax of a thing
11. "nation" — **ἔθνος** (*ethnos*): nations or ethnic groups; includes various nations, races, colors, or religious groups
12. "against" — **ἐπί** (*epi*): upon; superiority; pictures a crushing or subjugating force; a force that crushes or smashes; pictures a decimating force
13. "kingdom" — **βασιλεία** (*basileia*): a kingdom; a sphere of influence; ideology; a political realm

SYNOPSIS

After a time of ministry in Jerusalem, "…Jesus went out of the Temple and was walking away when his disciples came up and drew his attention to its buildings. 'You see all these?' replied Jesus. 'I tell you every stone will be thrown down till there is not a single one left standing upon another'" (Matthew 24:1-2 *JB Phillips*). Rocked by these words, the disciples were troubled and filled with questions concerning the end of the age.

Similarly, with all the craziness taking place in our world today, people are troubled and asking questions like, "How close are we to the end — when is the Rapture going to take place?" and, "What signs did Jesus give us to confirm His coming is near?" As believers living in the last of the last days, we need to know and understand what Jesus said, so we can recognize where we are on God's prophetic timeline and be ready for His return.

The emphasis of this lesson:

Wars, rumors of wars, commotions, nation rising against nation, and kingdom rising against kingdom are all signs Jesus prophesied would take place before His return and the end of the age. More signs will follow and increase in frequency and intensity, but rather than be troubled, we have been offered God's peace to guard our hearts and minds in Christ Jesus.

Questions About the End Times

Once the disciples were away from the crowds and had made their way to the Mount of Olives, "…the disciples came unto him privately, saying, Tell us, when shall these things be? and what shall be the sign of thy coming, and of the end of the world?" (Matthew 24:3)

There is nothing more fulfilling and rewarding than getting alone with Jesus! In those intimate moments, you can ask Him questions that are on your heart and hear the answers you need to hear. Indeed, the way He speaks to you in private is deeper and more personal than when you are with others, which is what the disciples experienced.

Essentially, the disciples asked Jesus, "Exactly when are these things going to happen? Tell us specifically — down to the smallest minuscule detail — what will be the major sign we'll see along the prophetic road to alert us that we're near to Your coming. When will You return and begin the process of dealing with the situation and putting everything in correct order. And tell us how we will know we've come to the consummation and the wrap-up of the age?"

We saw in Lesson 3 that the age we are living in is sometimes called the Church age or the age of grace. Biblically speaking, we are living in *the last days*, and according to Acts 2:15, it began shortly before 9 a.m. on the day of Pentecost in 33 AD. That is when God's Spirit was poured out on all flesh and the last days officially kicked off. That is the age we're living in right now and have been in for nearly 2,000 years. In this final sliver of time before Christ comes, we are going to see things no previous generation has seen.

Jesus Warned Against Being 'Deceived'

The very first words to come from Jesus' mouth in response to the disciples' questions is the foremost sign we will see, confirming we have entered the last of the last days, and that sign is *worldwide deception*. Matthew 24:4 says:

> **And Jesus answered and said unto them, Take heed that no man deceive you.**

We learned in our previous lesson that the words "take heed" are a form of the Greek word *blepo*, which means *watch*, *listen*, or *pay attention*. Jesus used this word *blepo* to jar and jolt His listeners, which includes us. It is as if He was saying, "Listen up! Throw your shoulders back, hold your head up high, and really pay attention to what I'm about to say. Take heed that no man deceive you."

The word "deceive" is a form of the Greek word *planao*, which pictures *deception* or *a moral wandering*. It depicts a person (or nation) who has veered from a solid path as a result of wandering morally. Jesus used this word to prophesy that at the very end of the age, society is going to morally wander off track and veer away from the solid path of moral truth on which they once walked.

We're living in a day when a large part of the world has gone "woke," and some people have wandered so far off track that now they don't even know what gender they are. When a person can't definitively discern his or her own gender, something is drastically wrong. Who would have imagined we would experience what we are seeing in our lifetime? It's deception (*planao*), and it's the mega-sign Jesus said we would see at the very end of the age.

This same Greek word *planao* — translated here as "deceive" — was also used in the agricultural world to depict a lost animal that couldn't find its way back home. It was so lost it couldn't find the path to get back to where it used to be. Hence, the use of this word here implies that society is going to get so far off track at the end of the age it will not be able to come home again. This extreme deviation and moral wandering is a requirement for the world to be primed, prepared, and modified to eventually receive and embrace the Antichrist.

FIVE ADDITIONAL SIGNS JESUS GAVE US

After Jesus alerted us to the major sign of *worldwide deception*, He began to innumerate a list of signs we will see at the very end of the age before He comes. These include wars, rumors of wars, commotions, nation rising against nation, and kingdom against kingdom. All these things will be indicative that we have sailed to the very last port in time and there is no time remaining.

'Wars'

In Matthew 24:6, Jesus said, "And ye shall hear of *wars*...." At the time Jesus said this, the Roman-dominated world was filled with all kinds of wars and conflicts, but that was not what He was referring to. He said, "And ye *shall hear* of wars," which indicates He was speaking futuristically about the end of the age.

When Jesus said, "And ye shall hear," the word He used for "hear" is the Greek word *akouo*, which means *to hear with the ear* and is from where we get the word *acoustics*. We are living in a time where we have instant access to news all the time. On our phones, our computers, and our TVs, we are constantly hearing about "wars," which is the Greek word *polemos*, a word that describes *armed conflicts*, such as *battles, fights, skirmishes, and large-scale conflicts*. The fact that this word is plural indicates that there are going to be multiple battles and conflicts occurring simultaneously across the planet.

'Rumors of Wars'

In addition to wars, Jesus said we would hear of "rumors of wars." The key to understanding this sign is in knowing the meaning of the word "rumors." In Greek, it is the word *akoe*, which is the word for *the human ear*. This word is describing *something heard in the ear*; hence, *a rumor*. The last days generation will have an earful of news and information about events occurring around the world. A better translation for "rumors of wars" would be, "You'll hear in your ears the sound of all kinds of *battles, fights, skirmishes, and large-scale conflicts* happening regionally and worldwide." This word "rumors" signifies an ear "buzzing" with information.

To be clear, Jesus never said we would personally see all these wars, revolts, and disturbances. He said we would *hear* about them. The Greek could literally be translated, "You will continually hear and hear and hear and hear," and it presents the idea of a nonstop flow of information. At the very end of the age, news of wars will be so abundant that we will feel like our ears are ringing with the sound of war. Jesus was prophesying that an earful of information regarding wars will be one of the foremost signs that the finality of the age is approaching.

Don't Be 'Troubled'

Immediately after Jesus alerted us to the occurrence of "wars and rumors of wars," He said, "…See that ye be not troubled: for all these things must come to pass, but the end is not yet" (Matthew 24:6). The word "troubled" in this verse is the Greek word *throeo*, and it describes *an inward fright that causes one to be filled with worry, anxiety, or fear*. It also depicts *worry and inward anxiety resulting from outward events that keep occurring repeatedly*.

Think about the typical response to hearing about all the armed conflicts, skirmishes, and battles in the world and in our nation. How do people react when they hear of missiles being launched, nuclear subs entering the area, or attack drones being released? They become filled with worry, anxiety, and fear. That's what the enemy wants, but Jesus said, "Don't be filled with worry or fear." Why? Because "…All these things must come to pass, but the end is not yet" (Matthew 24:6).

Notice the word "end" that Jesus used. In Greek, it is the word *telos*, and it describes *the ultimate conclusion or climax of a thing*. This verse tells us that even though *wars* and *rumors of wars* are major signs that confirm the wrap up of the age is near, they are not the ultimate sign that we have reached the very, very end of time.

'Commotions'

Luke's gospel reiterates what Jesus said in Matthew 24:6 but adds an additional sign. Luke 21:9 records Jesus as saying, "But when ye shall hear of wars and *commotions*, be not terrified: for these things must first come to pass; but the end is not by and by." The word "commotions" here is the Greek word *akatastasia*, and it describes *instability* or *something that is out of control*. It is the picture of *upheaval*, *anarchy*, or *turbulent upheavals of a societal, political, or militaristic nature*.

Without question, we are eyewitnesses to anarchy and societal upheavals all around us. Yet Jesus said that when you hear of such instability and upheavals, "…Be not terrified…" (Luke 21:9). In Greek, the word "terrified" is a translation of the word *ptoeo*, which describes *an inward fluttering, panic, or terror*. It means *to be terrorized* and denotes *a fright that results from something that startles or alarms*. Basically, it is the picture of *terrorism*. Thus, Jesus is saying, "Be not terrorized."

To help us better understand what Jesus is saying here, Rick read the following excerpt from his book *Signs You'll See Just Before Jesus Comes*:

> It's difficult to keep an accurate count of how many revolutions have occurred in recent years. There seems to be an unleashing of demonic forces into the earth with a fury that refuses to be pacified. If there has ever been a time when it felt like all restraints have been thrown off, it is now. To one observing the news, it appears as if the lid has been taken off Pandora's box — and we seem to be coexisting in a warring, terroristic environment that is unprecedented in scope.
>
> News media around the world regularly report incidents of terrorist activities. Reports from international intelligence agencies state that terrorism is escalating in an increasing number of nations. The Middle East as well as much of Europe and America lie marred in the global path of these bloody attacks. Middle-Easterners, Europeans, Asians, Americans, Africans, and Australians — people from nearly every part of the planet — have all felt the murderous effects of war and terrorism.
>
> The rise in this type of terrorist activity — 'commotions' that strike alarm in people's hearts — is unprecedented in our lifetime. But long ago when Jesus told His disciples about signs they would see to indicate the conclusion of the age, He exactly described the warring and terroristic activities that have become so commonplace in recent times.
>
> …Few anticipated what has transpired on the planet in such a relatively short period. The possibility of random terror attacks has come so close to our everyday lives that in many places — schools, grocery stores, malls, theaters, sports stadiums, and even churches — people are required to enter through metal

detectors to ensure their well-being against someone with an intent to kill.

When Jesus described key signs that would be evidence of the very end of the age, He prophesied that these very kinds of 'wars and rumors of wars, and commotions' would be another key to gauge where we are in time and to show that the age is drawing to a close.[1]

Yet regardless of what is going on, we are not to be filled with inner panic or terror. Jesus said, "…For these things must first come to pass; but the end is not by and by" (Luke 21:9). Again, the word "end" here is the Greek word *telos*, the same word used in Matthew 24:6. It describes *the ultimate conclusion or climax of a thing*. Jesus' use of this word lets us know that while "commotions" (terrorist activity) and "wars" are major signs that the wrap-up of the age is near, they are not the ultimate sign that we have reached the very, very end of time.

'Nation Shall Rise Against Nation'

Jesus continues to lay out the confirming, last-days signs in Matthew 24:7 where He says, "For nation shall rise against nation, and kingdom against kingdom…." First, notice the word "nation" used twice in this verse. It is the Greek word *ethnos*, which is the word for *nations* or *ethnic groups*. It includes various *nations*, *races*, *colors*, or *religious groups*. Thus, Jesus said that as we near the end of the age, *ethnic groups* will be seething so furiously they will rise against other *ethnic groups*, *races*, and *religious groups*.

This brings us to the word "against," which appears twice in Matthew 24:7. It is a form of the Greek word *epi*, and it means *upon*. It carries the idea of *superiority* and pictures *a crushing or subjugating force*; *a force that crushes or smashes*; *a decimating force*. The closer we get to the return of Christ and the wrap-up of the age, the more we will see ethnic groups try to crush and decimate other ethnic groups. These types of racial and religious conflicts will escalate on a scale no one has seen and spread across the planet like a disease. The fact is, we're seeing this take place all around us.

'Kingdom Shall Rise Against Kingdom'

In addition to nation rising against nation, Jesus said that "kingdom shall rise against kingdom" (Matthew 24:7). The Greek word for "kingdom" here is *basileia*, and it describes *a kingdom* or *a sphere of influence*. It also denotes *ideology* or even *something in the political realm*. Thus, we could translate Jesus' words, "Ideology shall rise against ideology," or "Political party shall rise against political party."

Here we see Jesus prophesied that political parties, alliances, and ideological factions will war against each other at the very end of the age, which is exactly what we see happening now. The incivility and violence we are witnessing between differing belief systems is unprecedented. Once more, the word "against" is used, which is the same Greek word *epi*. Its use here means that political parties and ideological factions are not just going to try to have the upper hand over the other. Instead, they are going to attempt to crush and subjugate one another with a decimating force.

Jesus said, when you've come to the very end of the age, these are the kinds of things you're going to hear about and see. Deception will be epidemic worldwide. Wars and rumors of wars will abound. Nation will rise against nation, and kingdom will rise against kingdom. Yet despite this increasingly volatile environment, it is not the end. More signs will follow and increase in frequency and intensity.

Here's the Good News!

Despite all these difficulties and the news reports that are buzzing in our ears, we do not have to be terrorized by any of it because the peace of God can keep our hearts and minds in Christ Jesus (*see* Philippians 4:7). Like the apostle Paul, we can entrust our lives into God's care and say as he said: "…For I know whom I have believed, and am persuaded that he is able to keep that which I have committed unto him against that day" (2 Timothy 1:12). Rather than worry and be anxious, we are to pray and surrender ourselves and our situations to God, and when we do, we can see the promise of God fulfilled: "And the peace of God, which passeth all understanding, shall keep your hearts and minds through Christ Jesus" (Philippians 4:7).

In our next lesson, we will continue our journey through Matthew 24 and discover what Jesus meant when He prophesied that *famines* and *pestilences* would also be signs marking the end of the age and His return.

STUDY QUESTIONS

> Study to shew thyself approved unto God, a workman that needeth not to be ashamed, rightly dividing the word of truth.
> — 2 Timothy 2:15

1. To combat the turmoil and trouble all around us, Jesus has given us His very own peace! Take a moment to reflect on what He said about peace in John 14:27 and 16:33. How do His words encourage you and provide you with hope? What do Psalm 119:165 and Isaiah 26:3 say are needed to have peace?

2. Philippians 4:7 says that God offers us "peace which passeth all understanding." The key to having and experiencing the protective, empowering peace from God is found by putting into practice the verses before and after verse seven. Take time to meditate on this passage, committing it to memory and allowing the Holy Spirit to root it deep inside you.

   Don't worry about anything; instead, pray about everything. Tell God what you need, and thank him for all he has done. Then you will experience God's peace, which exceeds anything we can understand. His peace will guard your hearts and minds as you live in Christ Jesus.

   …One final thing. Fix your thoughts on what is true, and honorable, and right, and pure, and lovely, and admirable. Think about things that are excellent and worthy of praise.
   — Philippians 4:6-8 *NLT*

PRACTICAL APPLICATION

> But be ye doers of the word, and not hearers only, deceiving your own selves.
> — James 1:22

1. When Jesus said, "For nation shall rise against nation, and kingdom against kingdom…" (Matthew 24:7), He was telling us that *ethnic and religious groups* will rise against *ethnic and religious groups*, and *ideology and political parties* will rise against *ideology and political parties* with *a crushing, smashing, or decimating force*. How does this meaning from the original Greek text expand your understanding of this prophetic

road sign Jesus gave us? How are you seeing this manifested in our world today?

2. In Matthew 24:6, Jesus said the last days generation would "hear of wars and rumors of wars," which carries the idea of having *ears buzzing with information* about wars and conflicts occurring all around the world. Knowing that the media has been weaponized to perpetuate strife, rivalry, anarchy, and violence in these last days, what practical steps can you take to guard yourself from being swept away by the chaos? As you answer, consider Psalm 101:3-4; Proverbs 4:23; Isaiah 26:3; Philippians 4:8; and Hebrews 12:1-3.

---

[1] *Signs You'll See Just Before Jesus Comes* by Rick Renner — pp. 54-55

LESSON 5

TOPIC

Are Shortages a Sign of the End?

SCRIPTURES

1. **Matthew 24:3** — And as he sat upon the mount of Olives, the disciples came unto him privately, saying, Tell us, when shall these things be? and what shall be the sign of thy coming, and of the end of the world?
2. **Matthew 24:7** — For nation shall rise against nation, and kingdom against kingdom: and there shall be famines, and pestilences....
3. **Proverbs 19:17** — He that hath pity upon the poor lendeth unto the Lord; and that which he hath given will he pay him again.
4. **Proverbs 21:13** — Whoso stoppeth his ears at the cry of the poor, he also shall cry himself, but shall not be heard.
5. **Proverbs 11:24-25** — There is that scattereth, and yet increaseth; and there is that withholdeth more than is meet, but it tendeth to poverty. The liberal soul shall be made fat: and he that watereth shall be watered also himself.

6. **Luke 21:11** — ...And [there shall be] pestilences; and fearful sights and great signs shall there be from heaven.
7. **Psalm 91:1** — He that dwelleth in the secret place of the most High shall abide under the shadow of the Almighty.
8. **Psalm 91:6** — Nor for the pestilence that walketh in darkness; nor for the destruction that wasteth at noonday.
9. **Psalm 91:10** — There shall no evil befall thee, neither shall any plague come nigh thy dwelling.
10. **Psalm 91:16** — With long life will I satisfy him, and shew him my salvation.

GREEK WORDS

1. "famines" — λιμός (*limos*): plural, meaning multiple famines; a scarcity of grain; deficits of all types, including financial deficits and shortages
2. "pestilences" — λοιμός (*loimos*): plural, meaning multiple pestilences; old diseases being reactivated or newly emerging diseases never seen before

SYNOPSIS

Do you have questions about the end times? Jesus' disciples did. Just after the Lord prophesied the destruction of the Temple, the disciples went to Him privately as He sat on the Mount of Olives and said, "...Tell us, when shall these things be? and what shall be the sign of thy coming, and of the end of the world?" (Matthew 24:3).

In the First Century, many Jews were seeking to learn about the end of the age as they looked eagerly for their long-awaited Messiah. It is much the same today, as believers wait for Christ's return to rapture the Church. As we've seen in our previous lessons, Jesus answered the disciples' questions, providing more than 20 signs that would authenticate and confirm the end of the age. The two additional signs we will examine in this lesson are *famines* and *pestilences*.

The emphasis of this lesson:

Famines and pestilences are also authenticating signs that Jesus said we will see before His return and the end of the age. Specifically, these words depict worldwide hunger and financial instability along with

widespread breakouts of old and new diseases. God wants us to be mindful to care for and give to those who are in need.

A Review of the First Six Prophetic Signs

Before we delve into the remarkable meanings of the words "famines" and "pestilences," let's take a few moments to quickly review all the signs we have examined so far. First and foremost, Jesus told us that *deception* will permeate the planet. Rather than hold to the truths of Judeo-Christian morals found in Scripture, society will abandon that path and embrace a level of immorality and insanity on a level we've never seen.

Jesus went on to prophetically forecast numerous additional signs He said we would see as we come to the end of the age. Here are the six signs we have covered in our first four lessons that appear in Matthew 24:4-7; Mark 13:5-8; and Luke 21:8-10:

1. **Worldwide deception** (Matthew 24:4; Mark 13:5-6; Luke 21:8)
2. **Wars** (Matthew 24:6; Mark 13:7; Luke 21:9)
3. **Rumors of wars** (Matthew 24:6; Mark 13:7)
4. **Commotions** (Luke 21:9)
5. **Nations rising against nations** (Matthew 24:7; Mark 13:8; Luke 21:10)
6. **Kingdoms rising against kingdoms** (Matthew 24:7; Mark 13:8; Luke 21:10)

Today, we are witnessing all six of these prophetic signs happening throughout the world. Deception is rampant in every sector of society. Wars abound and rumors of wars are buzzing in our ears continually. "Commotions," which would be better translated as "terrorism," are now affecting everyone on all continents. Likewise, "nations" — or *ethnic groups* — rising against nations and "kingdoms" — or *ideologies* and *political systems* — rising against kingdoms is an everyday occurrence.

'Famines' Are Another Major Sign

What else did Jesus say we would see as we near the time of His coming and the end of the age? He said there will be *famines, scarcities, economic woes, pestilences,* and *diseases*. The Bible captures these five additional signs within the words "famines" and "pestilences," which we will see as we examine the original Greek text. Although humanity has dealt with all these issues since the fall of man, Jesus prophesied that as we come to the end of the age, they are going to increase in frequency and intensity.

In Matthew 24:7, Jesus declared:

> **For nation shall rise against nation, and kingdom against kingdom: and there shall be famines, and pestilences....**

Notice the word "famines" in this verse. It is the Greek word *limos*, which is plural in form, signifying *multiple famines*. Normally, when we hear the word famine we think of a lack of food, which is certainly true, but it is much more than that. This word *limos*, which signifies multiple famines, also describes *a scarcity of grain* as well as *deficits of all types*, including *financial deficits and shortages*.

When we look at famines in the typical sense, which is a lack of food resulting in starvation, the statistics are staggering. Consider these findings from Rick's research that he included in his book *Signs You'll See Just Before Jesus Comes*:

> **According to a report from *2016 World Hunger and Poverty Facts and Statistics*, more than 250,000 people die every year around the world from hunger and hunger-related causes. Another shocking report is that between 250,000 to 500,000 children become blind each year due to vitamin deficiency caused by extreme undernourishment — and half of those die within a year of their blindness....**

> **Think of the famines that have purged millions of people from the planet in various parts of the world — even in our lifetime. The images of starving children and adults have been paraded before us on television and other media to bring the stark reality of this suffering to the forefront of our minds....**[1]

Thankfully, there are many wonderful ministries and charitable organizations that are providing food to the hungry and clean water to people all over the world, many of whom have no access to water. Friend, if you have clean water and food, you have more than what many people have. Although you may not have access to everything you want, you do have access to what you need. Tragically, there are people in other parts of the world who have no water or food at all, and many of them are suffering from malnutrition and starvation. Altogether, there are more people suffering right now than ever before.

Rick continued reading from his book:

> ...In many parts of the world, the lack of food and clean water — or the lack of any water at all — is an unimaginable crisis. Despite the wonderful efforts by many charitable organizations, the problems associated with hunger, malnutrition, and disease as a result of no water or dirty water has grown worse in recent years.
>
> Currently our planet has a population of [over 8] billion people. According to the Food and Agriculture Organization of the United Nations, approximately 1 in 9...suffer from chronic undernourishment. That means all these people lack the food necessary to maintain normal health. To help you understand the approximate size of that number, think of the population *of the entire European continent* — and then add to that the populations of California and Texas *combined*![2]

The number of people who are suffering from undernourishment, starvation, and a lack of water is unthinkable. Most of us take for granted the fact that we have easy access to nearby grocery stores and the resources needed to stop whenever we want and pick up food or enjoy a meal at a local restaurant. Let this be a Holy Spirit-inspired reminder to give to those who are in need.

God Calls Us To Give to Those in Need

Jesus said that at the very end of the age, famines would multiply in number and be amplified in intensity. This is a major last-days sign, and we are seeing this take place right before our eyes. Proverbs 19:17 says:

> **He that hath pity upon the poor lendeth unto the Lord; and that which he hath given will he pay him again.**

When you give to those who are destitute, you're lending to the Lord, and He will repay you for it. Another sobering verse to keep in mind is Proverbs 21:13, which says:

> **Whoso stoppeth his ears at the cry of the poor, he also shall cry himself, but shall not be heard.**

This passage lets us know that if we don't pay attention to the poor and to those who are suffering, it will get us in trouble later when we need help ourselves. Like with everything else in life, the law of sowing and reaping is always in effect: "…For whatsoever a man soweth, that shall he also reap" (Galatians 6:7).

Another great passage to take seriously and live your life by is Proverbs 11:24-25. It says:

> **There is that scattereth, and yet increaseth; and there is that withholdeth more than is meet, but it tendeth to poverty. The liberal soul shall be made fat: and he that watereth shall be watered also himself.**

People who "scattereth and increaseth" are those who give generously to others in need and are blessed with more. In contrast, people who "withholdeth" are those who are stingy and unwilling to help others who are suffering lack. The Bible says those who act in such a way are headed for poverty.

Friend, it is in your best interest to listen to the voice of the Holy Spirit and give to those who are in need as He prompts you — especially in this time when hunger, starvation, and famine are so intense around the world.

Whether it's supporting a ministry that digs water wells in foreign countries, giving funds to a local foodbank, or leaving a good tip for a single mom who's serving as a waitress, you will be blessed when you look for and seize opportunities to "scatter your financial seed" into the lives of those in need. God says if you'll do that, He will see to it that you increase. That's what is meant by Proverbs 11:25, which says, "The liberal soul shall be made fat: and he that watereth shall be watered also himself." God is going to see to it that you're taken care of when you help take care of others.

'Famines' Also Indicate Financial Instability

What is interesting about the word "famines" in Matthew 24:7, the Greek word *limos*, is that in addition to it describing a lack of food, it also denotes *a scarcity of grain*. This is important because in the First Century when Jesus was saying these things, economies were based *on grain*. If a person had a lot of grain, he was considered financially well off. If a person had a shortage of grain, he was seen as lacking and heading for a really bad financial year. Indeed, when there was a deficit of grain, it caused scarcity on every level.

For this reason, the Roman Empire strove to always maintain a good relationship with Egypt, because Egypt was the breadbasket of the Roman Empire. As long as Rome had access to the grain of Egypt, Rome was in good shape. But if Egypt had a plague or a famine and there was a shortage of grain or no grain at all, it shook the finances of the entire Roman Empire. Hence, this word "famines" (*limos*) inherently carries the idea of *financial deficits and shortages*. Jesus used this word in Matthew 24:7 to prophesy a scarcity of grain or widespread hunger in the last days as well as financial deficits or shortfalls in world markets that would affect the whole globe.

Moreover, this word *limos* can also describe *financial woes* such as financial shakings that would be repeated again and again. The reason we know this is a recurring issue is because in Greek, the word *limos* is plural, describing an event that happens again and again. Thus, in Matthew 24:7, Jesus was prophesying that financial instability would become more and more pronounced as we come closer to the end of the age.

'Pestilences' Are the Prophetic Sign of Old and New Diseases

Jesus identifies that along with famines, *pestilences* are another major sign marking the end of the age. In Luke 21:11, He informs us that there will be "famines and pestilences." In Greek, the word for "pestilences" is the medical term *loimos*, which is plural, meaning *multiple pestilences*. So rather than just indicating one pestilence, Jesus is alerting us to the emergence of multiple pestilences at the end of the age. "Pestilences" (*loimos*) describes *old diseases being reactivated* or *newly emerging diseases never seen before.*

Rick addresses this issue in his book *Signs You'll See Just Before Jesus Comes*:

> **The planet is already being hard-hit with multiple diseases that are decimating populations all over the world. Even if cures exist, medicines and supplies to deal with the avalanche of disease spreading throughout the human race are often in short supply.**
>
> **In addition to normal strains of disease that medical science regularly combats, today science is struggling to fight the onslaught of *newly emerging infectious diseases*. These are often**

actually old diseases that have had life breathed into them again. Such reemerging diseases have the potential to affect massive populations across the earth. Cures for these are frequently more difficult to find as new strains of the diseases become more powerful, and as a result, larger numbers of people are put at risk....

The U.N.'s *World Health Organization* (WHO) states that many potential epidemic and pandemic pestilences already exist in latent states. This means many life-threatening diseases are lying dormant and could be awakened at any moment to swiftly invade the human race. If even one or two of these epidemics became activated and found a way into the world's population, what could happen in a very brief period of time is unthinkable. The mere thought of this possibility has scientists and the medical world in a constant state of urgency.

...Professionals predict that directly before us will be the emergence of new infectious diseases and that the reemergence of 'old' diseases will have a significant impact on health. A number of factors will influence this development: travel and trade, microbiological resistance, human behavior, breakdowns in health systems, and increased pressure on the environment. Social, political, and economic factors that cause the movement of people will increase contact between people and microbes, and environmental changes caused by human activity all will contribute to the spread of disease. The overuse of antibiotics and insecticides, combined with inadequate or deteriorating public health infrastructures, will hamper or delay responses to increasing disease threats.[3]

What you just read are the findings of medical professionals and scientists, not theologians, and they agree with what Jesus prophesied would take place at the very end of the age. He said there will be *loimos* — multiple pestilences — which are *old diseases being reactivated* and *newly emerging diseases never seen before*. This will happen more and more as His coming approaches and the Church age wraps up.

It's Time To Live in the Promises of Psalm 91

Jesus' prophetic forecast for increased famines and pestilences gives us good reason to become familiar with and begin to live in the promises of Psalm 91, which starts off by saying:

> **He that dwelleth in the secret place of the most High shall abide under the shadow of the Almighty.**
> — **Psalm 91:1**

Five verses later, the psalmist declared that those who dwell in the secret place of the Most High will not in any way be afraid of "…The pestilence that walketh in darkness; nor for the destruction that wasteth at noonday" (Psalm 91:6). Then in verse 10, we are promised: "There shall no evil befall thee, neither shall any plague come nigh thy dwelling."

The psalmist ended Psalm 91 in verse 16 by declaring:

> **With long life will I satisfy him, and shew him my salvation.**

Friend, we must learn to live under the shadow of the Almighty, where we have the Lord's protection from famine and financial hardships as well as from all forms of disease and pestilences. Living in the shadow of the Most High is the safest, most productive place for us to live.

In our next lesson, we will examine another sign Jesus gave us that will send shockwaves across the globe to announce that we've come to the close of the age.

STUDY QUESTIONS

> Study to shew thyself approved unto God, a workman that needeth not to be ashamed, rightly dividing the word of truth.
> — 2 Timothy 2:15

1. The Bible says that God is mindful of the poor, and He will not forsake them (*see* Isaiah 41:17). He offers very special blessings to those who imitate Him and care for the poor too. Take some time to meditate and reflect on these promises:
    - **The blessings of giving to the poor**: Psalm 41:1-3; Proverbs 14:21; 22:9; 28:27

- **What Jesus said about the poor**: Matthew 19:21; Luke 12:33; 14:13-14
- **How God views your kindness to the poor**: Proverbs 14:31; 19:17; Deuteronomy 15:7-11
- **What happens when you give**: Luke 6:38; Proverbs 11:24-25; Galatians 6:7-10

2. Our actions speak much louder than our words, especially when it comes to caring for the needy and the sick. The Bible says, "…Faith and works, works and faith, fit together hand in glove" (James 2:18 *MSG*). Take a few moments to read these sobering words from James, John, and Jesus, and jot down what the Holy Spirit impresses upon your heart about helping those who are hurting.
   - Matthew 25:34-40
   - James 2:15-18
   - 1 John 3:16-18

PRACTICAL APPLICATION

> But be ye doers of the word, and not hearers only, deceiving your own selves.
> —James 1:22

1. To stand against the outbreak of pestilences in these last days, you need to know what the Bible says about healing and walking in divine health. What scriptures do you know that declare God's desire and power to heal you and your family?

2. God Himself has said, "…He that hath my word, let him speak my word faithfully…" (Jeremiah 23:28). To help build your faith and arm yourself with ammunition from God's Word, take some time to look up these promises on healing and divine health and begin making them a part of your prayers for yourself, your family, and others.
   - **God wants us to be healthy**: 3 John 2
   - **Abiding in God's presence brings healing and protection**: Psalm 91 1-16; 103:3
   - **Obedience and worship bring God's healing**: Exodus 15:26; 23:25-26; Proverbs 3:7-8

- **Feeding on God's Word brings healing**: Psalm 107:20; Proverbs 4:20-22
- **Jesus' sacrifice brings healing**: Isaiah 53:4-5; 1 Peter 2:24
- **Prayer and honest confession bring healing**: James 5:14-16

3. People are God's highest priority. If you want to touch His heart, make helping people one of your highest priorities too. Pray and ask Him, *How can I make a difference in the lives of others now and for eternity? What would You like me and my family to do? Who would You like us to support, and how much would You like us to give?* Be still and listen carefully to how He leads you and begin to do it by faith.

---

[1] *Signs You'll See Just Before Jesus Comes* by Rick Renner — pp. 72-73

[2] *Signs You'll See Just Before Jesus Comes* by Rick Renner — p. 73

[3] *Signs You'll See Just Before Jesus Comes* by Rick Renner — pp. 83-85

LESSON 6

TOPIC

Shockwaves and the Second Coming

SCRIPTURES

1. **Matthew 24:3** — And as he sat upon the mount of Olives, the disciples came unto him privately, saying, Tell us, when shall these things be? and what shall be the sign of thy coming, and of the end of the world?
2. **Matthew 24:7** — For nation shall rise against nation, and kingdom against kingdom: and there shall be famines, and pestilences, and earthquakes, in divers places.
3. **Luke 21:11** — And great earthquakes shall be in divers places, and famines, and pestilences; and fearful sights and great signs shall there be from heaven.

GREEK WORDS
1. "when" — ποτέ (*pote*): exactly when; indicates specific information
2. "what" — τι (*ti*): minute, minuscule detail; exactly; explicitly
3. "sign" — σημεῖον (*semeion*): a marker or sign used to alert a traveler to where he is on a road; authenticating marks or specific signs
4. "coming" — παρουσία (*parousia*): to be present; a technical expression for the royal visit of a king or emperor; the arrival of one who alone has the authority to deal with a situation and put things in correct order
5. "end" — συντέλειας (*sunteleias*): the closure, the summation, or wrap-up of the age
6. "world" — αἰῶνος (*aionos*): not the world itself, but the age
7. "earthquakes" — σεισμός (*seismos*): plural, multiple earthquakes; a lot of seismic activity
8. "great" — μεγάλοι (*megaloi*): a multiplicity of things; refers to size or quantity
9. "fearful sights" — φόβητρον (*phobetron*): monstrous events; scary events; used by ancient Greeks to describe monsters
10. "from" — ἀπό (*apo*): from; directly out of

SYNOPSIS

After Jesus informed us of the prophetic signs of worldwide deception; wars and rumors of wars; commotions; nations rising against nations and kingdoms against kingdoms; famines; and pestilences, He added *earthquakes* to the list along with something extremely bizarre — "fearful sights and great signs…from heaven" (Luke 21:11). What did He mean by that? Let's explore an aspect of the Greek that has even puzzled translators for many years.

The emphasis of this lesson:

Jesus prophesied in Matthew 24:7 and Luke 21:11 that in the last of the last days, increased seismic activity, including vast numbers of earthquakes, will take place globally. He also said we'd see monstrous things descending directly out of the heavens. These are major signs that Christ's return and the wrap up of the age is near.

A REVIEW OF MATTHEW 24:3

Matthew 24 describes a time when Jesus and His disciples were at the Temple marveling at its beauty. When the Lord prophesied that a time would come when not one stone would be left upon another, the disciples were dumbfounded. They then made their way down and across the Kidron Valley and up to the panoramic and prophetic view of Jerusalem from the Mount of Olives. The Bible says:

> **And as he [Jesus] sat upon the mount of Olives, the disciples came unto him privately, saying, Tell us, when shall these things be? and what shall be the sign of thy coming, and of the end of the world?**
>
> — Matthew 24:3

At that time in history, and during the preceding intertestamental period, there was a great fascination with the end of the age and *eschatology, the study of the end times*. Keep in mind that the Jewish people were dominated under harsh Roman rule, and they were looking for the long-awaited Messiah to come and free their nation.

Today, many believers are asking some of the same questions. "How close are we to the end of the age? When is Jesus coming to rapture His Church? And what signs will we see before His return?" Just as there is much speculation about prophecy today, there was a great deal of conjecture back then as well.

In Lessons 1 and 2, we examined six important words in Matthew 24:3 that we need to understand. They are: "when," "what," "sign," "coming," "end," and "world." Let's review their meaning once more by looking at the disciple's questions.

'WHEN shall these things be?'

In Greek, the word "when" is the word *pote*, which means *exactly when* and indicates *specific information*. The use of this word here is the equivalent of the disciples saying, "*Exactly when* will these things take place? We don't want a general answer; we want you to tell us specifically when what you said is going to happen."

'WHAT shall be the sign of Your coming?'

The word "what" here is the little Greek word *ti*, which describes *the most minute, minuscule detail*. Its use here was the equivalent of the disciples saying, "Jesus, we want You to tell us the bare facts and give us the most *minute, explicit details* regarding the sign of Your coming." Again, they didn't want general information.

Give us the SIGN, Lord'

The word "sign" in Matthew 24:3 is the Greek word *semeion*, and it describes *a marker or sign to alert a traveler to where he is on a road*. It is an *authenticating marker* or *road sign* you would see as you are travelling from one destination to another.

Rick gave the example of how he and his wife Denise live about seven and a half miles outside the city of Moscow, which is where their offices and their TV studio are located. When Rick and Denise travel to their office, the environment near their home is one of pastures, small neighborhoods, and forested land. As they take the road toward the city, the surrounding environment begins to change. Pastures and small homes give way to larger structures and industrial buildings, followed by even taller buildings that become a more packed, congested area.

All along the way, there are little road signs that tell them where they are on the road and how far they must go before they enter the city. Eventually, they cross a major highway called MKAD, and once they cross that road, there's a big sign that says *Moscow*. That sign lets travelers know that they're no longer traveling toward Moscow — they've *entered* the city. Without the signs, no one would know where they are on the road.

In the same way, the disciples asked Jesus, "What are the prophetic markers or signs we're going to see as we journey down the road to the end of the age?" By using this word "signs" — the Greek word *semeion* — the disciples were saying, "Lord, what changes are we going to see as time moves forward? How will we know we are close to the end of the age?" Interestingly, the text says they just asked for one sign, but Jesus gave them more than 20 signs to let them know exactly where they were on the road to the end of the age.

'What sign will confirm your COMING is near?'

The disciples specifically wanted to know the sign of Jesus' "coming." The Greek word for "coming" here is *parousia*, which literally means *to be present alongside*. It describes the coming or presence of the Lord.

Some argue that this word *parousia* only describes the Second Advent of Christ, which takes place at the very end of the seven-year Tribulation, but that is not the case. A careful study of its use in the New Testament reveals that it is used interchangeably to describe both the rapture of the Church and the Second Coming of Christ, and the way to know how *parousia* is being used depends on the context of surrounding verses.

This word *parousia* was a technical expression for *the royal visit of a king or emperor or the arrival of one who alone has the authority and power to deal with the situation and put everything in correct order*. Indeed, when the Rapture takes place, the power of God is going to begin to be released in a way never before seen to deal with the ungodly world. For seven years, God's wrath will be poured out to shake the world and to wake Israel to the reality that Jesus is indeed the Messiah. At the end of the seven-year Tribulation, Jesus will return to the earth and put all things back in order.

'When is the END of the WORLD?'

The last thing the disciples asked Jesus was what the sign would be to confirm "the end of the world" (Matthew 24:3). That is how their words are translated in the *King James Version*, but it is a very poor translation. In Greek, the word "end" is *sunteleias*, and rather than describing THE END, it describes *the closure, culmination, or wrap-up of something*.

Equally important is the word "world," which is not the word *gaius*, the term for *the earth*, or *kosmos*, the word for the *organized systems of the world*. Instead, it is the Greek word *aionos*, which means *the age*. When we pull together the meaning of all these words, we see that the disciples were asking: "Lord, tell us exactly when these things are going to happen. We don't want a general answer. We want to know explicitly when these things shall be. Please tell us — down to the smallest detail — what will be the road marker on the prophetic road — the primary sign — to let us know Your coming, when you're going to return and deal with everything wrong and set everything right, and of the culmination of this age is here."

Essentially, that is what the disciples were asking Jesus, and He answered their questions, giving them not just one but multiple signs He said we would see before His coming and the end of the age.

A Review of the First 11 Prophetic Signs

In Lessons 1 through 5, we examined 11 of the signs Jesus gave to alert us to the fact that His return and the wrap up of the age is very near. Here are the authenticating markers we can expect to see take place and the scripture passages where they appear:

1. **Worldwide deception** (Matthew 24:4; Mark 13:5,6; Luke 21:8)
2. **Wars** (Matthew 24:6; Mark 13:7; Luke 21:9)
3. **Rumors of wars** (Matthew 24:6; Mark 13:7)
4. **Commotions** (Luke 21:9)
5. **Nations rising against nations** (Matthew 24:7; Mark 13:8; Luke 21:10)
6. **Kingdoms rising against kingdoms** (Matthew 24:7; Mark 13:8; Luke 21:10)
7. **Famines** (Matthew 24:7; Mark 13:8; Luke 21:11)
8. **Scarcities** (Matthew 24:7; Mark 13:8; Luke 21:11)
9. **Economic woes** (Matthew 24:7; Mark 13:8; Luke 21:11)
10. **Pestilences** (Matthew 24:7; Luke 21:11)
11. **Diseases** (Matthew 24:7; Luke 21:11)

Today, we are seeing all 11 of these prophetic signs occurring across the globe. Each incident, which now seems to be happening one on top of the other, is another "contraction" the world and humanity are experiencing that is bringing us closer and closer to the end of the Church age and the birth of the Tribulation.

An Increase in 'Earthquakes' Is a Major Last-Days Sign

The next three signs Jesus said we would see before He comes and the last days end are *catastrophic events*, *monstrous developments*, and *signs from the heavens*. We find these mentioned in Matthew 24:7; Mark 13:8; and Luke 21:11.

Look again at Matthew 24:7:

> **For nation shall rise against nation, and kingdom against kingdom: and there shall be famines, and pestilences, and earthquakes, in divers places.**

Notice the word "earthquakes." In Greek, it is the word *seismos*, which is where we get the word *seismograph*. It is plural, so it indicates *multiple earthquakes* or *a great deal of seismic activity*, including both earthquakes and volcanic eruptions.

In Luke 21:11, Jesus' words are recorded a bit differently:

> **And great earthquakes shall be in divers places, and famines, and pestilences; and fearful sights and great signs shall there be from heaven.**

Again, we see the word "earthquakes," which is the same Greek word *seismos*, indicating *multiple earthquakes* or *a great deal of seismic activity*. But in Luke's account, he adds the word "great." He says, "...*Great* earthquakes shall be in divers places..." (Luke 21:11). The word "great" is the Greek word *megaloi*, and it describes *a multiplicity of things*. It can refer to *size* or *quantity*, and in this verse, it probably applies to both. Thus, there's going to be an increase in the quantity of earthquakes and also in the intensity or severity of the quakes themselves.

Rick addresses this in his book *Signs You'll See Just Before Jesus Comes*:

> **The words 'great earthquakes' in Greek literally mean *great seismic activity*. The word used in the original language can depict something *large* in size, or it can also mean *numerous* in quantity. Furthermore, Jesus stated that these earthquakes will occur in 'divers places.' This means the earth will be touched globally by increased seismic activity toward the end of the age.**
>
> **Scientific record demonstrates that earthquakes are a part of the geological history of the earth. But Jesus was not giving a history of the earth when He spoke about earthquakes in Matthew 24:7 and Luke 21:11. He was forecasting *what will happen* in a condensed period of time at the very end of the era. According to Jesus, increased seismic activity will take place globally and a vast number of earthquakes will be felt in various places across the earth.**

> Recent reports made by the *United States Geological Survey* (USGS) estimate that several million earthquakes occur in the world each year. However, many of these go undetected because they affect remote areas or register very small magnitudes....
>
> In Luke's gospel, Jesus said that there would be 'great' seismic activity as the time of His return approached. We can infer from this verse of Scripture that 'great' may mean *great quantity*. Approximately 500,000 smaller earthquakes are occurring every year. We know that even now, the earth is trembling with *great numbers* of earthquakes.[1]

The apostle Paul wrote prophetically about this seismic activity in his letter to the Roman believers. He said, "It is plain to anyone with eyes to see that at the present time all created life groans in a sort of universal travail" (Romans 8:22 *JB Phillips*). This same verse in *The Message* says, "All around us we observe a pregnant creation. The difficult times of pain throughout the world are simply birth pangs." But the day is coming when the birth pains will end, and the Spirit of God will deliver us from this earth and into the presence of Jesus for eternity!

Jesus Prophesied That We Would See 'Fearful Sights'

In addition to the catastrophic seismic activity, there is another sign Jesus gave us, and it is only found in Luke 21:11:

> And great earthquakes shall be in divers places, and famines, and pestilences; and *fearful sights* and *great signs shall there be from heaven.*

The Greek word for "fearful sights" is a very strange term. In fact, it is so bizarre that translators didn't know what to do with it, so they translated it "fearful sights." It is the Greek word *phobetron*, a word that was well-known in the Greek world to describe *monsters* — scary creatures that are abnormalities. Although it can also describe *monstrous events* or *scary events*, a literal translation for the word *phobetron* is *monsters*. That is how it was used by ancient Greeks.

What in the world did Jesus mean when He said there will be the appearance of monsters at the end of the age? Well, as we noted, it could describe monstrous events. Rick speaks of this possibility in his book *Signs You'll See Just Before Jesus Comes*:

> **One previously unimaginable possibility that has arisen in the modern age is the advent of a *horrific scientific or technological development*.**
>
> **The idea that technology could unleash profound devastation comes as no surprise in the modern era....**[2]

Prior to the use of the atomic bomb in WWII, no one knew the extensive devastation such technology would cause. Similarly, few know the new kinds of technology that is out in the world today and of what it is capable. Maybe "fearful sights" — the Greek word *phobetron* — is referring to something like that.

In a certain sense, we're living in a day of monsters. People are doing all kinds of things to their body — even trying to change their biological gender through drugs and surgical procedures. They are literally attempting to redefine who God made them to be. If we were able to transport a person from a hundred years ago into the present and put him in a shopping center so he could observe people today, he might feel as though he were surrounded by monsters.

Nevertheless, it must be said that in the world of Greek readers, when they saw the word *phobetron* in Luke 21:11, they weren't thinking about technology. They were thinking about monsters. Time will tell exactly what Jesus meant.

They Will Come 'From Heaven'

Jesus said something else very interesting regarding these "fearful sights." He said, "...Fearful sights and great signs shall there be *from heaven*" (Luke 21:11). The word "from" here is very important. In Greek, it is the word *apo*, which describes *something coming directly out of the skies* or *directly out of the heavens*.

Obviously, there could be a lot of conjecture about what this means. Some people think this will be an asteroid or a meteor. There is certainly a lot of scientific talk about that these days. At the same time, it's possible that these "fearful sights and great signs" are connected to the UFOs and UAPs that so many are talking about. Indeed, these things are appearing in increased numbers, descending directly from the heavens. So much so that even Congress is talking about it.

Exactly what they are we don't know. Yet Jesus said that when we come to the very end of the age, there's going to be the appearance of monstrous things coming directly from the heavens, and their appearance, along with increased catastrophic seismic activity, will be signs that His coming and the end of the age is near.

In Lesson 7, we will continue our study of Matthew 24 and see what other signs Jesus said we would see just before He returns.

STUDY QUESTIONS

Study to shew thyself approved unto God, a workman that needeth not to be ashamed, rightly dividing the word of truth.
— 2 Timothy 2:15

1. In Matthew 24:8, Jesus likened the prophetic signs of His coming and the end of the age to "the beginning of sorrows," which in the Greek describes the *birth pains* an expectant mother experiences as she enters the labor-and-delivery phase for her baby. How does Romans 8:22 compare with what Jesus said in Matthew 24:8?
2. Why has creation been subjected to death and decay? (*See* Genesis 3:17-18; Romans 5:12; and Romans 8:20.)
3. Read Romans 8:21 What miracle did Paul prophesy is going to occur in the earth? (*See* also 2 Peter 3:13 and Revelation 21:1.)

PRACTICAL APPLICATION

But be ye doers of the word, and not hearers only, deceiving your own selves.
— James 1:22

1. A great surge in seismic activity — which includes earthquakes and related volcanic eruptions — is one of the major prophetic signs Jesus gave to signify His coming and the end of the age. Are we seeing this take place in the world today? For an eye-opening look at how earthquakes have increased in frequency and intensity over the past few decades and in recent years, visit earthquake.usgs.gov and the interactive earthquake map at seismo.berkeley.edu. How does seeing

this scientific data confirm Jesus' prophetic words and excite you about His soon appearance?

2. According to Jesus, the last days generation is going to see "fearful sights and great signs from heaven" (*see* Luke 21:11). Prior to this teaching, had you ever heard that such events were coming? Why do you think Jesus left this particular sign as such a mystery?

_____

[1] *Signs You'll See Just Before Jesus Comes* by Rick Renner — pp. 100-102

[2] *Signs You'll See Just Before Jesus Comes* by Rick Renner — p. 103

LESSON 7

TOPIC

Deception. Wars. Earthquakes.

SCRIPTURES

1. **Matthew 24:3** — And as he sat upon the mount of Olives, the disciples came unto him privately, saying, Tell us, when shall these things be? and what shall be the sign of thy coming, and of the end of the world?
2. **Matthew 24:8** — All these are the beginning of sorrows.
3. **Acts 2:14-20** — But Peter, standing up with the eleven, lifted up his voice, and said unto them, Ye men of Judaea, and all ye that dwell at Jerusalem, be this known unto you, and hearken to my words: For these are not drunken, as ye suppose, seeing it is but the third hour of the day. But this is that which was spoken by the prophet Joel; And it shall come to pass in the last days, saith God, I will pour out of my Spirit upon all flesh: and your sons and your daughters shall prophesy, and your young men shall see visions, and your old men shall dream dreams: And on my servants and on my handmaidens I will pour out in those days of my Spirit; and they shall prophesy: And I will shew wonders in heaven above, and signs in the earth beneath; blood, and fire, and vapour of smoke: The sun shall be turned into darkness, and

the moon into blood, before the great and notable day of the Lord come.
4. **Matthew 24:9** — Then shall they deliver you up to be afflicted….
5. **Matthew 24:10** — And then shall many be offended, and shall betray one another, and shall hate one another.
6. **Luke 21:12** — But before all these, they shall lay their hands on you, and persecute you, delivering you up to the synagogues, and into prisons, being brought before kings and rulers for my name's sake.
7. **Luke 21:13** — And it shall turn to you for a testimony.
8. **Luke 21:14-15** — Settle it therefore in your hearts, not to meditate before what ye shall answer: For I will give you a mouth and wisdom, which all your adversaries shall not be able to gainsay nor resist.

GREEK WORDS
1. "sorrows" — **ὠδίν** (*oodin*): birth pains; pain of childbirth; contractions; the pain necessary to open up or to introduce something new
2. "afflicted" — **θλῖψις** (*thlipsis*): describes a crushing or debilitating situation; affliction; tribulation; trouble; great pressure; crushing pressure; suffocating pressure; a horribly tight, life-threatening squeeze
3. "kill" — **ἀποκτείνω** (*apokteino*): slaughter; massacre; butcher; ruthlessly kill; torture; outright slaughter; can denote the giving of a death sentence
4. "hated" — **μισέω** (*miseo*): hate; abhor; to find something utterly repulsive; a deep-seated animosity; intense hatred; repugnance; to find something objectionable; to feel disgust toward something; repulsion; a deep-seated aversion; not just a case of dislike; it is a case of actual hatred
5. "offended" — **σκανδαλίζω** (*skandalidzo*): scandal; scandalous; offend
6. "betray" — **παραδίδωμι** (*paradidomi*): to deliver or to hand something over to someone else; to betray by delivering

SYNOPSIS
The fact that you are alive on the earth at this point in history is no accident. The Bible says God made "…all nations of men to settle on the face of the earth, having definitely determined [their] allotted periods of time and the fixed boundaries of their habitation (their settlements, lands, and abodes)" (Acts 17:26 *AMPC*). Your time of birth and your life were ordered by God

Himself, and in His book, every day was written down before even one of them took place (*see* Psalm 139:16). As you seek Him and receive the strength of His Holy Spirit daily, you will have everything you need to navigate these last days and walk through any difficulty victoriously!

The emphasis of this lesson:

Jesus said worldwide persecution of Christians is a sign that we've come to the end of the age. Before He returns, the Church will experience crushing or debilitating situations in various forms and in various places around the world, including overwhelming pressures, deep-seated hatred, betrayal, imprisonment, and in some cases death.

A Quick Review

As we have seen in our study, Jesus' disciples were earnestly seeking to know about the end times. After He prophesied that the Temple would one day be utterly destroyed, they looked for a chance to question Him and learn the timing of that event and its connection with the end of the age.

Matthew 24:3 says, "And as he [Jesus] sat upon the mount of Olives, the disciples came unto him privately, saying, Tell us, when shall these things be? and what shall be the sign of thy coming, and of the end of the world?"

The disciples asked for *one* sign, but Jesus gave them *multiple* signs, demonstrating the fact that when we get alone with Jesus, He'll answer our questions and tell us many other things we didn't even know to ask Him. Here are the 14 signs we have covered so far:

1. **Worldwide deception**

2. **Wars**

3. **Rumors of wars**

4. **Commotions**

5. **Nations rising against nations**

6. **Kingdoms rising against kingdoms**

7. **Famines**

8. **Scarcities**

9. **Economic woes**

10. **Pestilences**

11. **Diseases**

12. **Catastrophic events**

13. **Monstrous developments**

14. **Signs from the heavens**

These signs of the end of the age and Christ's coming were spoken by Jesus Himself and are recorded in Matthew 24; Mark 13; and Luke 21. What's interesting is that in Matthew 24:8, Jesus said, "All these are the beginning of sorrows." The word "sorrows" here is the Greek word *oodin*, which describes *birth pains*. When a pregnant woman draws near to her time of delivery, she begins to have *contractions*. That is what Jesus compares all these prophetic signs to that will mark His coming and the end of the age.

The 'Last Days' Are From Pentecost to the Rapture

We understand from history that Jesus died on the Cross and was resurrected in 33 AD. At 9:00 a.m. fifty days later, after Jesus' resurrection, the day of Pentecost took place (*see* Acts 2:15), and the Holy Spirit was poured out upon believers, giving birth to the Church. The outpouring of the Spirit is what triggered the period that the Bible calls *the last days*, and we've been living in that timeframe for the last 2,000 years.

Some people call this era *the Church age*, which is accurate because we are living in the age of the Church. Other people call this time *the age of grace*, which is also true because it is the period in which God's grace has been poured out on mankind. Thank God for His amazing grace!

When we reach the end of this current age, the rapture of the Church is going to take place. Make no mistake: the Rapture is not a fantasy. It is a real event that is really going to happen. The Bible says Jesus is going to descend from Heaven into the clouds just above the earth. As He gives a mighty shout, the trump of God will sound, and with the voice of the archangel, the dead in Christ — those who put their faith in Him — will be brought back to life! Immediately after they're resurrected and raised into the air, we who are alive and remain will be caught up (raptured) to meet the Lord in the air with them (*see* 1 Thessalonians 4:17).

Once we're snatched up into Heaven, we will attend the Marriage Feast of the Lamb and be brought individually before the judgment seat of Christ. These two events will take place during a seven-year period, during which back on earth, those who have rejected Jesus will experience what the Bible calls the Tribulation, a time of unprecedented trouble and difficulty.

We Are Experiencing 'Birth Pains'

So when the disciples asked Jesus, "…What shall be the sign of thy coming, and of the end of the world?" (Matthew 24:3), they were not asking about the entire 2,000-year last-days period. They were asking about *the very end of the age*, or the very end of the 2,000-year Church age. They wanted to know the sign that would confirm that we are at the very end.

After answering their questions, Jesus referred to the signs as the beginning of "sorrows" (*see* Matthew 24:8), which is the Greek word *oodin*. In other words, they are like the birth pains of a woman who is about to deliver a baby. Essentially, Jesus said, "When you come to the very, very end of the last days and things are wrapping up, all these signs will begin to take place, and they will be like the contractions of a woman in labor." These birth pains or contractions are necessary to open up or to introduce something new.

On the program, Rick recalled the time when Denise was pregnant with their first son Paul, "When she had her first birth pain, she wasn't really sure it was even a contraction. She said, 'Rick, I just felt something, and I think it was a contraction.' Before long, the guessing game was over. She knew she was having contractions, and they began to come faster, stronger, and closer together until, finally, the contractions were one on top of the next. A short time later, she delivered our first son into the world."

Jesus used this word *oodin*, the Greek word for *birth pains*, to tell us that as we come to the very end of the age, the world at large will begin to experience occasional episodes of trouble. As time goes by, these difficulties are going to increase in number, frequency, and intensity, just like a woman having contractions as she prepares to have her baby. One troubling event after another will occur until they begin to pile one on top of the other.

Friend, that is what we are seeing right now. All these signs that Jesus prophesied are happening so fast and so frequently that it is hard to keep track of everything. Just 50 years ago, these history-making events were occurring every now and then, and when they did, they were big news. Today, these things are happening simultaneously and are so numerous that people are nearly numb to how earth shattering these events are.

We're living in a time like no other, and these non-stop "contractions" are all signs that we're drawing very close to the conclusion of this age when the rapture of the Church will take place and the birth of the next age — the Tribulation — will occur. For true believers who are snatched away into Heaven, it is going to be glorious! But for the ungodly left behind on the earth, those seven years of tribulation are going to be devastating beyond words.

The 'Day of the Lord' Is Coming

As we mentioned, the day of Pentecost marked the beginning of the last days. For 2,000 years now, we have been in this prophesied period of time. In Acts 2:14-20, Peter gave an overview of this timeframe from the day of Pentecost all the way to the end of the age:

> **But Peter, standing up with the eleven, lifted up his voice, and said unto them, Ye men of Judaea, and all ye that dwell at Jerusalem, be this known unto you, and hearken to my words: For these are not drunken, as ye suppose, seeing it is but the third hour of the day. But this is that which was spoken by the prophet Joel; And it shall come to pass in the last days, saith God, I will pour out of my Spirit upon all flesh: and your sons and your daughters shall prophesy, and your young men shall see visions, and your old men shall dream dreams: And on my servants and on my handmaidens I will pour out in those days of my Spirit; and they shall prophesy: And I will shew wonders in heaven above, and signs in the earth beneath; blood, and fire, and vapour of smoke: The sun shall be turned into darkness, and the moon into blood, before the great and notable day of the Lord come.**

Notice the last verse, which says "…the sun shall be turned into darkness, and the moon into blood, before the great and notable day of the Lord come." The phrase "notable day of the Lord" is a reference to the seven-year

Tribulation, which is also known as "the day of the Lord." This time of God's wrath will be so horrific, the inhabitants of the earth — rich and poor, slave and free — will hide themselves in the rocks and caves, crying out to the mountains and rocks saying, "...Fall on us, and hide us from the face of him that sitteth on the throne, and from the wrath of the Lamb: For the great day of his wrath is come; and who shall be able to stand?" (Revelation 6:16-17).

Sign #15: Worldwide Persecution

Jesus continued to provide prophetic signs that confirm our closeness to the end of the age in Matthew 24:9 where He said, "Then shall they deliver you up to be afflicted…." Here we see sign number 15, which is *worldwide persecution*. Depending on where you live, you may not see or hear about people dying for their faith because there are religious rights and liberties in place to protect the citizens. But in other parts of the world, many people are suffering for their faith even as you read this. In fact, right now, more than 200 million Christians are suffering to some degree for their faith.

In his book *Signs You'll See Just Before Jesus Comes*, Rick addresses this:

> **These are serious days. We cannot neglect the fact that approximately 75 percent of the world right now lives in situations that are precarious for believers. In fact, it is only a small fraction of the world that knows no Christian persecution.**
>
> **…Also, according to the United States Department of State, Christians in more than 60 countries face persecution from their governments or surrounding neighbors simply because of their belief in Jesus Christ.**
>
> **The U.S. Department of State confirms this statistic that believers in more than 60 nations of the world face persecution because of their Christian faith….**
>
> **[More than 200,000,000] Christians are suffering from some kind of persecution for their faith…. By definition, these persecutions include harassments, pressures, hardness of life, and hostility — oftentimes violent and even leading to death — for calling oneself a Christian. Types of persecution range from**

pressure from family and community to government-imposed afflictions to violent acts carried out by terrorist groups.

…The Bible prophesies that persecution in some form will come to the Church at the very end of the age — Jesus Himself said it would. It is time for the Christian community to be wide awake and united in order to spiritually withstand the powers of wickedness that will attempt to "modify" the Church and nullify its effectiveness in the last of the last days.[1]

When Jesus said that believers would be delivered up to be "afflicted" (Matthew 24:9), He used the Greek word *thlipsis*, which describes *a heavy-pressure situation*. It was first used to denote an act of torture whereby a person would be tied with ropes, laid on his back, and told to reject his faith or to confess to a crime. If that person would not comply, a large stone would be lowered down by a rope and held above him, and he would be told again to recant or reject his faith. If he refused, the huge, heavy stone would continue to be lowered until, finally, he would feel the full pressure of it upon him. Once more, he would be told to admit to a crime or to reject his faith, and if he would not comply, the rope holding the huge stone would be severed, and the stone would fall and crush the accused.

That is a clear picture of the word *thlipsis*: *a crushing or debilitating situation*. It is the picture of *affliction*; *tribulation*; *trouble*; *great pressure*; *crushing pressure*; *suffocating pressure*; or *a horribly tight, life-threatening squeeze*. Jesus said that this kind of pressure is going to come to believers all over the world in the last of the last days.

Believers Will Be 'Hated and Killed'

In fact, Jesus goes on in Matthew 24:9 to say, "…[They] shall kill you…." That word "kill" is the Greek word *apokteino*, which describes *butchery*. It means *to slaughter, massacre, butcher, ruthlessly kill*, or *torture*. It describes *outright slaughter* and can denote *the giving of a death sentence*. You may not know of any Christians in your neighborhood being butchered for their faith, but there are Christians being slaughtered all over the world today, especially in countries in Africa and the Middle East. Indeed, many believers around the world are living under a death sentence — more than 200 million are suffering.

Jesus said that in addition to being "afflicted" and "killed," believers will be "hated of all nations" for His name's sake (Matthew 24:9). The word "hated," which is repeated twice in Matthew 24, is the Greek word *miseo*, and it means *to hate, to abhor*, or *to find something utterly repulsive*. It is *a deep-seated animosity, intense hatred*, or *repugnance*. It carries the idea of finding something objectionable or feeling disgust toward something; a repulsion. It is *a deep-seated aversion* or *actual hatred*, not just a case of dislike.

Jesus used this word *miseo* to describe the deep-seated aversion, repugnance, and intense hatred that society will have toward Christians at the end of the age. Rather than just dislike believers, people in the world will actually have a feeling of disgust and be repulsed by them, and this will be evident globally at the end of the age.

Offense Will Give Way to Betrayal

Another indicator of the soon coming of Christ and the wrap-up of all things is cited by Jesus in Matthew 24:10. He said, "And then shall many be offended…." The word "offended" here is the Greek word *skandalidzo*, which means *scandal, scandalous*, or *to offend*. It is from where we get the word *scandal*, and it is so indicative of the age in which we're living right now.

Jesus prophesied that at the end of the age, the mutinous, lost world will become so negative about Christians that they will find them to be offensive and even scandalous. They will say things like, "How dare you say Jesus is the only way! Who are you to say there is only one gender? You are so bigoted and narrow-minded!" Society will view Christians who stand firmly on God's Word to be scandalous.

But that's not all. In Matthew 24:10, Jesus added, "…[Many] shall betray one another, and shall hate one another." The word "betray" is also very important. It is the Greek word *paradidomi*, which means *to deliver* or *to hand something over to someone else*. Thus, people will betray believers by delivering them over to others.

The Legal System Will Be Weaponized Against Christians

Then for a second time, Jesus said, "…[Many] shall hate one another" (Matthew 24:10). Here again is the word "hate," the Greek word *miseo*, describing *a deep-seated animosity, intense hatred*, or *repugnance*. People in society will find Christians to be so repulsive and objectionable that Jesus said, "...They shall lay their hands on you, and persecute you, delivering you up to the synagogues, and into prisons, being brought before kings and rulers for my name's sake" (Luke 21:12).

What do synagogues have to do with the persecution of believers? Well, in the First Century, when Jesus spoke this, the community synagogue also served as the local court for the legal system. Therefore, when Jesus said that people would deliver believers up to the synagogues, He was actually saying they're going to turn Christians over to the legal system. Hence, He prophesied the *weaponizing* of the legal system.

When speaking about the believers who are brought before the courts, Jesus said, "...It shall turn to you for a testimony" (Luke 21:13). In other words, the situation of persecution will be turned into a golden opportunity to testify of Jesus. If this should happen to you, Jesus added, "Settle it therefore in your hearts, not to meditate before what ye shall answer: For I will give you a mouth and wisdom, which all your adversaries shall not be able to gainsay nor resist" (Luke 21:14-15).

So as we approach the end of the age and the coming of Jesus, worldwide persecution will be in full swing. This is already a reality and a major sign that we're coming close to the very end. In response, we need to pray regularly and fervently for our brothers and sisters in Christ who are in jeopardy. We need to do whatever we can to help them, whether that's giving finances or praying for them to be bold in their witness for Christ and provided with God's power, protection, and provision in their situations.

In our next lesson, we will look at another major last-days sign Jesus gave us, which is the emergence of false prophets.

STUDY QUESTIONS

Study to shew thyself approved unto God, a workman that needeth not to be ashamed, rightly dividing the word of truth.
— 2 Timothy 2:15

1. After Jesus alerted us of the persecution we would experience for His name's sake, He told us not to worry and that He would help us. What powerful promise did He make in Matthew 10:19-20; Mark 13:11; and Luke 12:11-12 and 21:14-15? Why do you think He repeated this

promise so many times? How do His words give you confidence and hope?

2. The topic of persecution is not pleasant. That is why God offers many words of encouragement to those who remain faithful to Him. Take time to reflect on what He promised in these verses and tell how they encourage you to obediently press on in faith and trust Him to keep you in His care.

- Psalm 31:23
- Proverbs 2:8
- Isaiah 41:10-16; 43:1-3
- Matthew 10:28-32
- John 16:33
- 2 Timothy 4:18
- Hebrews 13:5-6

PRACTICAL APPLICATION

> But be ye doers of the word, and not hearers only, deceiving your own selves.
> —James 1:22

1. In this lesson, we learned that worldwide persecution of believers is a major sign that we're in the last of the last days. Have you personally experienced any type of persecution at the hands of family members, coworkers, or others? If so, briefly share what you endured. How has this experience brought you closer to Christ and strengthened your faith?

2. In the First Century, Christians tenaciously held on to the belief that Jesus is *the* way, *the* truth, and *the* life (*see* John 14:6). Do you believe this foundational truth, or do you find yourself wavering in your faith? Are you experiencing external pressure to be more inclusive, adaptable, and open-minded of those with differing spiritual views? What has been your response to this pressure?

3. Hebrews 13:3 (*NLT*) says, "Remember those in prison, as if you were there yourself. Remember also those being mistreated, as if you felt their pain in your own bodies." Take time to pray for brothers and sisters in Christ who are suffering for their faith. In whatever practical and spiritual ways you would want to be helped if you were suffering,

intercede for them. Pray for them to be filled with the power of the Holy Spirit to be a bold witness for Christ right where they are.

---

[1] *Signs You'll See Just Before Jesus Comes* by Rick Renner — pp. 117, 120, 124

LESSON 8

TOPIC
False Prophets — What Did Jesus Say?

SCRIPTURES

1. **Matthew 24:3** — And as he sat upon the mount of Olives, the disciples came unto him privately, saying, Tell us, when shall these things be? and what shall be the sign of thy coming, and of the end of the world?
2. **Matthew 24:11** — And many false prophets shall rise, and shall deceive many.
3. **1 Timothy 4:1** — Now the Spirit speaketh expressly, that in the latter times some shall depart from the faith, giving heed to seducing spirits, and doctrines of devils.

GREEK WORDS

1. "what" — τι (*ti*): minute, minuscule detail; exactly; explicitly
2. "coming" — παρουσία (*parousia*): to be present; a technical expression for the royal visit of a king or emperor; the arrival of one who alone has the authority to deal with a situation and put things in correct order
3. "end" — συντέλειας (*sunteleias*): the closure, the summation, or the wrap-up of the age
4. "world" — αἰῶνος (*aionos*): not the world itself, but the age
5. "many" — πολλοὶ (*polloi*): vast multitudes; many

6. "false prophets" — ψευδοπροφήτης (*pseudoprophetes*): false revelators; cult leaders; cultic movements
7. "deceive" — πλανάω (*planao*): a moral wandering
8. "many" — πολλοί (*polloi*): vast multitudes; many
9. "expressly" — ῥητῶς (*rhetos*): unmistakably; vividly; pictures something spoken clearly or something that is unquestionable, certain, and sure
10. "latter" — ὕστερος (*husteros*): later; pictures the ultimate end or the very last of something
11. "shall depart" — ἀφίστημι (*apistemi*): to change positions; a slow, methodical departure
12. "depart" — ἀφίστημι (*aphistemi*): a compound of ἀπό (*apo*) and ἵστημι (*histimi*); ἀπό (*apo*) means away, and ἵστημι (*histimi*) means to stand; compounded, they form the word ἀφίστημι (*aphistemi*), which means to stand apart from; to distance one's self from; to step away from; to withdraw from; or to shrink away from; it is from this very Greek word that we derive the word apostate or apostasy
13. "giving heed" — προσέχω (*prosecho*): to embrace; giving one's full attention to something with the intent to embrace it
14. "seducing" — πλανάω (*planao*): to wander; pictures deception or a moral wandering
15. "doctrines" — διδασκαλία (*didaskalia*): well-packaged teaching that is applicable to lifestyle
16. "depart" — ἀφίστημι (*apistemi*): to change positions; a slow, methodical departure
17. "giving heed" — προσέχω (*prosecho*): to embrace; giving one's full attention to something with the intent to embrace it

SYNOPSIS

Jesus informed us of the many specific signs we'll see before He comes to rapture the Church at the end of this age. One major sign He prophesied was the emergence of false prophets (*see* Matthew 24:11). After warning us not to be deceived, He said, "For many will come claiming to be the Messiah and will lead many astray" (Matthew 24:5 *TLB*). In this lesson, Rick explains the meaning of *false prophets*, providing several modern-day examples and how to avoid being taken by their schemes.

The emphasis of this lesson:

The rise of false prophets and false religious movements will grow exponentially just before Jesus comes. He declared that multitudes of pretend, bogus prophets would emerge and deceive many people. We are seeing this take place through the proliferation of Islam, Hinduism, various eastern religions, and cult movements like Mormonism.

The Disciples Sought Answers About the End of the Age

Returning to our foundational verse in Matthew 24:3, we read, "And as he [Jesus] sat upon the mount of Olives, the disciples came unto him privately, saying, Tell us, when shall these things be? and what shall be the sign of thy coming, and of the end of the world?" There amidst the panoramic view of the city of Jerusalem, with the Temple Mount glistening in the sunlight, the disciples asked Jesus to disclose to them the exact, explicit sign of His coming and the very end of the age.

We saw in previous lessons that the word "coming" is a translation of the Greek word *parousia*, which means *to be present*. But it was also a technical expression for the royal visit of a king or emperor and the arrival of one who alone has the authority to deal with a situation and put things in correct order. Jesus is the only One who has both the authority and power to correct everything that is wrong in this world, which is what He will do when He comes.

In the *King James Version*, when it talks about "the end of the world," the wording is a poor translation. The word "end" is the Greek word *sunteleias*, which describes *the closure*, *the summation*, or *the wrap-up*, and the word "world" in Greek is *aionos*, which describes *the age*, not the physical world itself.

Thus, the disciples weren't asking about when the world would end because that is never going to happen. Although the Bible does say the earth is going to be refined and transformed by fire in the future (*see* 2 Peter 3:7,12), it will never pass away. This present age will come to an end, and it will conclude with the rapture of the church. That event will trigger and initiate the seven-year Tribulation. Therefore, what the disciples were asking was, "Lord, how will we know when we've come to the very end of the age — what will be the sign?"

15 Last-Days Signs Jesus Gave Us So Far

Although the disciples only asked for one sign, Jesus gave more than 20. Here are the 15 signs we have examined in the first seven lessons that all point to and indicate the nearness of Jesus' coming and the end of the age:

1. **Worldwide deception**
2. **Wars**
3. **Rumors of wars**
4. **Commotions**
5. **Nations rising against nations**
6. **Kingdoms rising against kingdoms**
7. **Famines**
8. **Scarcities**
9. **Economic woes**
10. **Pestilences**
11. **Diseases**
12. **Catastrophic events**
13. **Monstrous developments**
14. **Signs from the heavens**
15. **Worldwide persecution**

You don't need to be an expert to notice that we are seeing all of the above signs in our world today. Just turn on the news or scan the Internet headlines, and you will quickly see reports of all these things taking place across the globe. This brings us to the next major prophetic marker signifying the end of the age and Christ's coming.

Sign #16:
The Emergence of 'False Prophets'

As Jesus continued providing prophetic signs of the last of the last days, He said, "And many false prophets shall rise, and shall deceive many"

(Matthew 24:11). First, note the words "shall deceive." This tells us Jesus was speaking futuristically. At that moment in time, there were false prophets around, but Jesus was answering the disciples' question about what would happen at the end of the age. He said many false prophets *shall arise* in that timeframe.

Next, notice the word "many" in Matthew 24:11, which appears twice. It is the Greek word *polloi*, which means *many* and describes *vast multitudes*. Thus, *vast multitudes* of false prophets will arise to deceive *multitudes* of people at the end of the age.

This brings us to the words "false prophets," which are a translation of the Greek word *pseudoprophetes*. It is a compound of two words: the word *pseudo* and the word *prophetes*. The word *pseudo* means *false, fake*, or *phony*, and the word *prophetes* is the term for *prophet*. When these words are joined to form the word *pseudoprophetes*, the new word refers to a *pretend prophet*, a *bogus prophet*, or *one who claims revelation and divine inspiration but is not sent by God*. He or she asserts to speak by supernatural revelation, but in fact that person, Jesus said, is *pseudo* or false.

Essentially, the words "false prophets" in Greek would better be translated *false revelators*. It depicts cult leaders and can even portray the idea of *false religious movements*. Jesus said these false revelators "...shall rise, and shall deceive many" (Matthew 24:11). What's interesting is that the word "deceive" is the same Greek word we see multiple times throughout Matthew 24. It is the word *planao*, which describes *a moral wandering*.

Jesus' use of this word *planao* (deceive) in connection with the word *polloi* (many) implies that there is going to be a multitude of voices that arise at the end of the age that are going to change the Gospel, attempting to make it say something that it doesn't say. Certain individuals will claim it's okay to compromise the standards of Scripture and will encourage God's people to morally wander off the path of biblical truth.

In his book *Signs You'll See Just Before Jesus Comes*, Rick addresses this:

> **The truth is that there are multitudes of individuals and religious organizations that claim to be divinely authorized and inspired. But they are *false* in that they do not represent the truth of the Bible. Some of them might preach and adhere to *some* Bible truth. But the core Bible doctrines of *salvation through Christ alone, His death and resurrection*, and *His***

present-day position and ministry are tainted and erroneous — to the great detriment of the followers of these groups.

…[Most false] movements had an originator, or founder, who claimed some "special" visitation from God, whether by an angel, a dream, or some other supernatural means. He or she received so-called revelation that either does not exist within the Bible or that alters the meaning of the Bible.

…The common denominator of the majority of false religions is they had a founder — a so-called prophet, seer, or leader. From the time of their respective supernatural experiences, these leaders began teaching their unique revelations to people who would blindly believe and follow them. Over the years, aggregated *millions* have pledged their allegiance — which has included the resources of their money and their time — to these cults and false leaders.

This has happened just as Jesus forecasted when He spoke to His disciples in Matthew 24:11. If you are amazed at the strange concoctions of partial truths, false religions, and cults that exist in the world today, just take these things as a sign that we are bumping into the end of the age! Jesus prophesied that such individuals and organizations would emerge in large numbers in the very last days.[1]

Examples of False Religious Movements

Without question, false religions have multiplied rapidly in our day, each one presenting its own version of truth. This is exactly what Jesus prophesied — that many false revelators will appear on the scene at the very end of the age. The truth is we are surrounded by numerous false religions in every corner of the globe. Here is a sampling of some of the more widely known cults and false religions:

- Baha'i Faith
- Buddhism
- Scientology
- Hinduism
- Unitarianism

- **Christian Science**
- **Islam**
- **Universalism**
- **Unitarianism**
- **Edgar Cayce**
- **Jehovah's Witnesses**
- **Mormonism**
- **Sun Myung Moon (Unification Church)**
- **Eastern cults (Hare Krishna, etc.)**
- **New Age Religions**

In Matthew 24:11, Jesus noted that when we see vast multitudes of false prophets — which includes multitudes of individuals and religious organizations who have a twisted interpretation of the Gospel and God's Word — we can know that we are bumping into the end of the age. All of these are cults and fake religious movements that are in the world. But what about *in the Church*? What has the Holy Spirit forewarned would take place among believers?

Some 'Shall Depart From the Faith'

One of the most disturbing last-days signs is that this departure from the truth will also take place inside the Church. In First Timothy 4:1, the apostle Paul confirmed that deception will infiltrate the Church. Writing under the inspiration of the Holy Spirit, he said, "Now the Spirit speaketh expressly, that in the latter times some shall depart from the faith, giving heed to seducing spirits, and doctrines of devils."

There are several important words to understand in this passage, starting with the word "expressly." This is the Greek word *rhetos*, and it describes *something that is spoken unmistakably, vividly, or undisputedly*. It pictures *something spoken clearly or something that is unquestionable, certain, and sure*. Hence, in the strongest, clearest, most indisputable language, the Holy Spirit declared that "…in the latter times some shall depart from the faith…." (1 Timothy 4:1).

The word "latter" is also significant. In Greek, it is the word *husteros*, which in addition to meaning *later*, it pictures *the ultimate end* or *the very last of something*. And the word "times" is a form of the Greek word *kairos*, which describes *a season of time*. Thus, the Holy Spirit speaks vividly, indisputably, and beyond the shadow of a doubt that when we come to the very end of the age, "…some shall depart from the faith…." (1 Timothy 4:1).

Notice the phrase "shall depart." It is a translation of the Greek word *aphistemi*, which is a compound of the words *apo* and *histimi*. The word *apo* means *away* and carries the idea of putting distance between you and something else. And the word *histimi* means *to stand*. When compounded to form the word *aphistemi*, it means *to stand apart from* and pictures one who steps away from what he once believed. In fact, instead of just stepping away or withdrawing from it, he puts distance between himself and his former faith. This word *aphistemi* is from where we derive the English words "apostate" and "apostasy."

The Holy Spirit indisputably, explicitly, and beyond the shadow of a doubt declared that at the end of the age, when we come to the final sliver of time, *apostasy* is going to take place. People who once held tightly to and stood by the truth of God's Word are going to step away from what they once believed and put distance between them and "the faith."

In the original Greek text, the word *faith* has a definite article with it, which means it is not faith in general — it is THE "faith" or *the clear, sound teaching of Scripture*. Paul said this departure (apostasy) from the clear, sound teaching of Scripture will happen because people are "…giving heed to seducing spirits, and doctrines of devils" (1 Timothy 4:1).

'Giving Heed to Seducing Spirits and Doctrines of Demons'

The phrase "giving heed" is a translation of the Greek word *prosecho*, a compound of the words *pros* and *echo*. *Pros* means *toward* and depicts closeness and intimacy, and the word *echo* means *to have*, *to hold*, or *to possess something*. When compounded to form *prosecho*, it means *to give one's full attention to something with the intent to embrace it*.

By using the word *prosecho* (giving heed), the Holy Spirit is letting us know that in the last of the last days, there will be people who were once grounded in God's Word that will turn their attention to something new. They will begin giving their devotion to something intriguing and tantalizing in order to embrace it, and this will result from the activity of *seducing spirits*.

Interestingly, the word "seducing" in Greek is a form of the word *planao*, the same word that appears repeatedly in Matthew 24 and throughout the New Testament that describes *a moral wandering*. Demon spirits are going to tempt people to abandon walking on the straight and narrow path of biblical truth in order to embrace a wider, more inclusive and less restrictive way of living that endorses every manner of lifestyle.

The Bible says this departure from the faith will be the work of *seducing spirits and doctrines of demons*.

The word "doctrines" is the Greek word *didaskalia*, which is from the word *didasko*, the term for *doctrine*. When *didasko* becomes *didaskalia*, it's no longer just doctrine. It is now *very well-packaged teaching that is applicable to lifestyle*. The use of this word lets us know that at the end of the age, the devil is not going to show up in a red skin suit with horns, a tail, and a pitchfork. Instead, he is going to peddle his perversion through well-polished people, bringing seducing ideas just like he did to Eve in the Garden of Eden. He's going to offer well-packaged information that will deceive people away from the straight and narrow path we're called to walk and onto a wider path that allows for moral wandering.

Putting It All Together

In review, First Timothy 4:1 in the *King James Version* says, "Now the Spirit speaketh expressly, that in the latter times some shall depart from the faith, giving heed to seducing spirits, and doctrines of devils." When we factor in the Greek meaning of the key words in this verse, we could translate it: "Now the Spirit speaketh expressly, emphatically, undeniably, and without question…."

In other words, what the Holy Spirit is describing here is not optional — it is definitely going to take place. The Holy Spirit then says:

> **…In the latter times, when we've come to the very end of the age and there's only a sliver of time left, some shall depart from the faith. That is, people who once stood firmly by the clear, sound teaching of Scripture will very slowly and methodically begin to change their position and move away from what the Bible teaches, putting distance between themselves and what they once believed and endorsed. Now they've taken a new position, and it's the result of giving heed to seducing spirits**

and doctrines of demons. They have turned their attention to hear something different.

Friend, in this day of great deception, you must be very careful what you listen to and watch. Feed on and get rooted in God's Word so that you can recognize and guard your heart against getting sucked into the deception of seducing spirits and doctrines of demons that would cause you to morally wander off course.

Satan is extremely cunning and is offering very well-packaged information that is quite convincing. This is happening right now in our day in unprecedented ways. The Internet and the airwaves are filled with fallacies that appear to be real but are nothing more than dressed up deception. This is a major sign that we have reached the very end of the age. Don't buy Satan's lies! Hold firmly to the truth, and keep your eyes focused on Jesus.

In our next lesson, we will examine the prophetic sign of *iniquity abounding* and how endurance will be needed to make it all the way to the end of this last-days season.

STUDY QUESTIONS

> **Study to shew thyself approved unto God, a workman that needeth not to be ashamed, rightly dividing the word of truth.**
> **— 2 Timothy 2:15**

In this day, when false prophets and false religions abound, we must be aware of what we're dealing with. Did you know that if you take all the religions of the world and put them in one group and then take Christianity and place it in a group by itself, something remarkable becomes visible:

1. **All World Religions Make These Two Claims:**
   - Jesus Christ is *not* the Son of God or God Himself.
   - Man can somehow work his way into right relationship with God to attain Heaven.

2. **Christianity Makes These Two Claims**:
   - Jesus Christ is the Son of God and God Himself.
     - Matthew 8:28-29, 14:31-33; and 26:63-64
     - Mark 1:1, 14:61-62

- John 17:1-3
- Romans 1:1-4
- Man *cannot* work his way into right relationship with God to attain Heaven. Therefore, God took on human form in the man Christ Jesus and paid the price for our sins, restoring us into right relationship with Himself.
  - John 14:6
  - Acts 4:12
  - Romans 3:20-24
  - Galatians 2:16
  - Ephesians 2:1-9
  - 1 Timothy 2:5-6

Invest some time looking up these scriptures that make clear these two foundational truths, and then commit them to memory.

PRACTICAL APPLICATION

> But be ye doers of the word, and not hearers only, deceiving your own selves.
> —James 1:22

1. What was your most memorable encounter with a false religion or false prophet? Which religious movement did you encounter? How did you respond to what you heard? How did you treat the people who shared the message?
2. How does the Bible specifically instruct us in First Peter 3:15 to prepare for encounters with unbelievers? And in what attitude should we do it?
3. In the last days, demon spirits are going to tempt people to abandon walking on the straight and narrow path of biblical truth in order to embrace a less restrictive way of living. The devil is going to peddle his perversion through well-polished people, bringing seducing ideas just like he did to Eve in the Garden of Eden. How will you guard against this and shine the light of truth in these last of the last days?

---

[1] *Signs You'll See Just Before Jesus Comes* by Rick Renner — pp. 131, 132, 134

LESSON 9

TOPIC
End-Time Pressure vs. Your Faith

SCRIPTURES
1. **Matthew 24:3** — And as he sat upon the mount of Olives, the disciples came unto him privately, saying, Tell us, when shall these things be? and what shall be the sign of thy coming, and of the end of the world?
2. **Matthew 24:12** — And because iniquity shall abound, the love of many shall wax cold.
3. **Matthew 24:13** — But he that shall endure unto the end, the same shall be saved.

GREEK WORDS
1. "iniquity" — ἀνομία (*anomia*): without law; lawlessness; a lawless attitude
2. "abound" — πληθύνω (*plethuno*): to increase to maximum capacity
3. "love" — ἀγάπη (*agape*): God's love
4. "many" — πολλοί (*polloi*): many; multitudes
5. "wax cold" — ψύχω (*psucho*): cold air; a breeze that cools or freezes
6. "endure" — ὑπομένω (*hupomeno*): a compound of ὑπό (*hupo*) and ὑμένω (*meno*); the word ὑπό (*hupo*) means under, and ὑμένω (*meno*) means to stay, to abide, or to remain in one's spot; to keep a position; to resolve to maintain territory gained; in a military sense, it pictures soldiers ordered to maintain their positions even in the face of opposition; to defiantly stick it out regardless of pressures mounted against it; staying power; hang-in-there power; the attitude that holds out, holds on, outlasts, perseveres, and hangs in there, never giving up, refusing to surrender to obstacles, and turning down every opportunity to quit; it pictures one who is under a heavy load but refuses to bend, break, or surrender because he is convinced that the territory, promise, or principle under assault rightfully belongs to him
7. "end" — τέλος (*telos*): the ultimate conclusion or climax of a thing

8. "saved" — **σῴζω** (*sodzo*): to heal, but conveys the idea of wholeness or salvation; wholeness in every part of life; a touch of salvation that brings delivering and healing power that results in wholeness; to deliver one's country from enemies; to protect, keep safe, or keep under protection

SYNOPSIS

As Jesus sat upon the Mount of Olives, He spoke to all His disciples — both then and now — and pointed a prophetic finger 2,000 years into the future, declaring the signs we could expect to see at the very end of the age. One thing He foretold was, "…Because iniquity shall abound, the love of many shall wax cold. But he that shall endure unto the end, the same shall be saved" (Matthew 24:12-13).

Friend, we are the ones living in the last of the last days. The Holy Spirit has "tagged" us to represent Christ in these final hours — a time in which the world seems to be morally spinning out of control. By renewing our minds with the truth and wisdom of God's Word, and receiving the supernatural empowerment of His Spirit, we can learn to live our life ablaze and avoid the love of God growing cold in our hearts.

The emphasis of this lesson:

Jesus said lawlessness will increase and flourish at the end of the age, and because of this lawless attitude, the *agape* love of believers for God and for one another will wax cold. To stay passionate in our love for Jesus and our love for others, we must abide in the truth of God's Word and stay close to the fire of the Spirit.

Jesus Gave Us Multiple Signs To Signify the End of the Age

The disciples were searching for answers regarding the wrap-up of the age and Christ's return. That's why they came to Him privately as He sat on the Mount of Olives and asked, "…Tell us, when shall these things be? and what shall be the sign of thy coming, and of the end of the world?" (Matthew 24:3).

We have learned from our previous lessons that what the disciples were wanting to know was what specific authenticating sign would mark the very end of the age and Jesus' coming. The number one sign the Lord gave them — and us — is *worldwide deception*. He then added more than 20 additional signs of which we have now covered 16, and they are:

1. **Worldwide deception**
2. **Wars**
3. **Rumors of wars**
4. **Commotions**
5. **Nations rising against nations**
6. **Kingdoms rising against kingdoms**
7. **Famines**
8. **Scarcities**
9. **Economic woes**
10. **Pestilences**
11. **Diseases**
12. **Catastrophic events**
13. **Monstrous developments**
14. **Signs from the heavens**
15. **Worldwide persecution**
16. **The emergence of false prophets**

Right now, all these things are taking place. They serve as authenticating markers on the prophetic road that indicate we are coming to the close of the current age, the timeframe the Bible refers to as *the last days*, also known as *the Church age* and *the age of grace*. At the close or consummation of this age, Jesus will return like a thief in the night to rapture the Church. That will initiate the next age, which the Bible calls the Tribulation.

Sign #17:
'Iniquity Will Abound'

In Matthew 24:12, Jesus prophesied two more signs that would be prevalent the last of the last days. He said, "And because iniquity shall abound, the love of many shall wax cold." Here we see that *iniquity abounding* is the next sign that the end is near and Jesus is about ready to come.

In Greek, the word for "iniquity" is *anomia*, which is from the word *nomas*, the word for *law*. But when you attach an "a" to the front of the word, it cancels or reverses the meaning. Hence, *anomia* means *without law* or *lawlessness*, which is what it describes in this verse.

This word *anomia* — translated here as "iniquity" — pictures people who have cast aside the law of God and say, "We've been there and done that. We don't want to live that way anymore. We want to be free from the restraints of God's instructions and the teachings of the Bible. It's outdated, and we don't believe it any longer. We want to forge our own brand-new path!" That's what iniquity or lawlessness (*anomia*) thinks and says.

In his book *Signs You'll See Just Before Jesus Comes*, Rick expounds on the meaning of iniquity:

> **In Greek, the word 'iniquity' actually describes *lawlessness*. A literal translation of this verse could be, '...Because *lawlessness* will abound, the love of many shall wax cold.' The word 'lawlessness' is *plural* in the Greek text, which tells us Jesus was foretelling a time when lawlessness would escalate around the world.**
>
> **...The word 'lawlessness'...refers to the actions of an individual, a group of people, a nation — or even an entire society or culture — that has chosen to live apart from God's laws and principles. Although this person or group previously followed biblical laws and principles *in general*, they elected to forge their own ways of doing things that are *not* founded on the principles of God's Word. Thus, they are *lawless*, or living by their own newly evolving principles that are not based on established truths so vividly portrayed in Scripture.**
>
> **...This collective rejection of God and His time-tested truths is confirmed by Paul in Second Thessalonians 2:3, where he described a great 'falling away' of people in the last days. Paul**

wrote, 'Let no man deceive you by any means: for that day shall not come, except there come a *falling away* first, and that man of sin be revealed, the son of perdition.'

In this verse, Paul prophetically described a falling away that will transpire in *society at large* at the very end of this age. In that hour, the 'mystery of iniquity' (v. 7), which has been working for some 2,000 years, will be unleashed *full steam* in an attempt to lead the entire planet into various forms of deception....

The words 'falling away' in Second Thessalonians 2:3 are used in the Greek Old Testament (Septuagint) to depict *a mass mutiny against authority*. But in this epistle to the Thessalonian church, they describe society revolting against the authority *of God Himself* at the conclusion of the age.

It is a fact that both Jesus and Paul prophesied that a great falling away *will* occur in the last days. The Bible describes it as a worldwide rebellion against God in society — across the planet.[1]

Jesus plainly stated that *lawlessness* (iniquity) will "abound" at the end of the age. In Greek, the word "abound" is *plethuno*, which means *to increase to maximum capacity*. The use of this word tells us that lawlessness will be a *big* problem, not a small one. This mass divergence or departure from the teaching of the Bible will escalate and proliferate at the end of the age and will reach maximum capacity across the planet. In increasing numbers, people will throw aside God's laws, choosing to make their own laws and rules and go in a new direction.

We are seeing this take place everywhere — in the judicial system, the education system, the halls of government, and in the entertainment industry in Hollywood. The world is going "woke," which essentially means society is no longer walking in the path and direction of the Bible. It is carving out its own new, "progressive" way of living.

Jesus said at the very end of the age, the entire planet will be impacted by this kind of thinking. The fact that we are witnessing this in our day is a major sign that we're colliding with the very end of the age. The only way to avoid going "woke" with the rest of the world is to determine to hold tightly to God's Word and make it the compass for your life.

Sign #18:
'The Love of Many Will Wax Cold'

Jesus went on to declare that because of this proliferating *lawless attitude*, "…The love of many shall wax cold" (Matthew 24:12). What the Lord is saying here is made quite clear in the original Greek text, especially with regards to the meaning of the word *love*.

In Greek, the word for "love" is *agape*, which describes *God's love*. The use of the word *agape* could only indicate the love of believers — a love we have toward God and toward fellow Christians. When Jesus said, "…The love of many shall wax cold" (Matthew 24:12), He was specifically talking about the love of believers waning toward God and toward others, and the reason it is waxing cold is because iniquity is abounding.

Just as Lot, Abraham's nephew, was vexed by the immoral thinking and behavior that surrounded him in Sodom, believers living in the last of the last days will be bombarded by immoral thinking and even teaching that is contrary to God's Word. The Bible states that this immoral mindset will have a detrimental effect on the agape love of God among "many." Here again we see the Greek word *polloi*, indicating a *vast multitude* of believers will be affected.

Jesus said this agape love will "wax cold." The phrase "wax cold" is a translation of the Greek word *psucho*, which describes *cold air* or *a breeze that cools or freezes*. At the very end of the age, there's going to be a cold breeze that blows through the Church that is going to cause people to become spiritually cold in their love toward God and each other. We are witnessing the effects of this today.

There are many people who don't attend church as they once did and people who are not as on fire for the Lord as they once were. Instead, they are compromising what they used to believe and adopting new mindsets that are more inclusive and more open-minded toward those practicing immoral behavior.

Although it's good to be open-minded, we shouldn't be so open-minded that our brains fall out! The flexibility in our thinking should never go against the Word of God. We must remain rooted and established in the never-changing standards of Scripture. [For more on this topic of staying rooted and grounded in Christ in these last days, it is recommended that you read Rick's book *How to Keep Your Head on Straight in a World Gone Crazy*.]

Those Who 'Endure' to the End Will Be Saved

Just after warning us that the love of many believers will grow cold, Jesus said, "But he that shall endure unto the end, the same shall be saved" (Matthew 24:13). The word "endure" is one of the most important words in the New Testament. It is a form of the Greek word *hupomeno*, a compound of the words *hupo* and *meno*. The word *hupo* means *under*, and *meno* means *to stay*, *to abide*, or *to remain in one's spot*. When these words are combined to form *hupomeno*, it means *to keep a position* or *to resolve to maintain territory gained*.

This word depicts a person who says, "*Meno!* — this is my spot, and I'm not moving or surrendering! I don't care how heavy the load gets or how hard it is. I've resolved that I'm not budging or moving. I'm going to stay right here where God placed me." Therefore, when Jesus says, "He that endures to the end," it is the equivalent of saying, "He who remains in the place that he knows is right to the end," or "He that keeps a position and resolves to maintain the territory gained to the end."

In a military sense, the word *hupomeno* pictures soldiers ordered to maintain their positions even in the face of opposition. It means to defiantly stick it out regardless of pressures mounted against it. It is *staying power* or *hang-in-there power*. It is *the attitude that holds out, holds on, outlasts, perseveres, and hangs in there, never giving up, refusing to surrender to obstacles, and turning down every opportunity to quit.* This word *hupomeno* depicts one who is under a heavy load but refuses to bend, break, or surrender because he is convinced that the territory, promise, or principle under assault rightfully belongs to him.

If you want to experience the saving, preserving, delivering power of God, you must stay put where He placed you and choose to withdraw from ungodly influences that numb you and cause God's love to wax cold. Likewise, you must stand by the teachings of Scripture and refuse to bend or back down from it. Regardless of what comes against you, you must not surrender, and you must turn down every opportunity to modify your faith to adapt to the world around you. That's what Jesus meant when He said, "But he that shall *endure* unto the end, the same shall be saved" (Matthew 24:13).

The key to experiencing the rewards of enduring is holding on and persevering until the *end*. This word "end" is the Greek word *telos*, which describes the *ultimate conclusion or climax of a thing*. Essentially, the disciples asked Jesus to give them the prophetic sign that would signify they had reached the very *end* of the age (*see* Matthew 24:3). Jesus' answer is certainly in line with what they asked.

What It Means To Be 'Saved'

Again, Jesus said that those who endure to the end, "…the same shall be saved" (Matthew 24:13). The word "saved" here is a form of the Greek word *sodzo*, which is the most important word in the New Testament for *salvation*. At the same time, it conveys so much more than just going to Heaven. It carries the idea of *salvation* and *wholeness in every part of life*. It is *a touch of salvation that brings delivering and healing power that results in wholeness*. It also signifies the idea of *delivering one's country from enemies*. Furthermore, it means *to protect, keep safe*, or *to keep under protection*. In context here, Jesus is saying, "If you'll stick with the Bible, it will enable you to be preserved and protected all the way to the end."

Friend, when you make the decision to stay put, even if the world around you changes and people ridicule you and call you all kinds of profane names, you will be saved. Christians have always been called names and persecuted in various degrees, and the end of the age will be no different. In fact, the opposition from society is going to become more intense because iniquity (*lawlessness*) will abound. Consequently, the agape love of God in multitudes of believers will wax cold as a chilling breeze blows through the Church.

Nevertheless, those who *endure* — those who say, "I'm not going to wander or move. I'm going to stand on God's Word and not deviate from what it teaches. I'm going to hold on, persevere, never budge, never give up, and stay locked into truth" — will be saved. They will be delivered, be healed, and experience God's power and wholeness in every area of their life. That's what the word "saved" — the Greek word *sodzo* — actually means.

In our final lesson, we will look closely at the final sign that must occur before Christ comes and the Church age ends.

STUDY QUESTIONS

> Study to shew thyself approved unto God, a workman that needeth not to be ashamed, rightly dividing the word of truth.
> — 2 Timothy 2:15

1. Believers in all generations sometimes struggle to keep their love for Jesus burning brightly, and the Church of Ephesus is a prime example of this. Read what Jesus said to them in Revelation 2:5. How can you personally apply Jesus' instructions to your own life?
2. Read what the apostle Paul wrote in First Timothy 4:14 and Second Timothy 1:6. How do you think these instructions relate to what the Bible says in First Corinthians 14:4; Ephesians 6:18; and Jude 20?

PRACTICAL APPLICATION

> But be ye doers of the word, and not hearers only, deceiving your own selves.
> — James 1:22

1. Jesus said *lawlessness* — choosing to live apart from God's laws and principles — will escalate across the planet at the end of the age. In what ways do you see this happening in society?
2. Be honest. With all the ungodly behavior and the departure from biblical truth taking place, have you become spiritually *numb*? Has God's *agape* love in you grown cold toward Him or toward other believers? If so, is it just the byproduct of our sinful society? Or is it the result of tolerating your own sin? Ask the Holy Spirit to show you the state of your heart (*see* Psalm 139:23-24). If you need to repent of sin and ask God to forgive you, take time to do that now.
3. To keep your fire for Jesus burning brightly in these last days, you must choose to stand firmly by the truth of God's Word and abandon ungodly influences that numb you and cause God's love in you to wax cold. Take time to pray, *Lord, are there any compromising or evil influences I need to pull away from? What can I adjust in my life to spend more time in Your Word and in Your presence?* Be still and listen. What is He showing you and asking you to do?

---

[1] *Signs You'll See Just Before Jesus Comes* by Rick Renner — pp. 139-141

LESSON 10

TOPIC
When the Gospel Goes Global

SCRIPTURES
1. **Matthew 24:3** — And as he sat upon the mount of Olives, the disciples came unto him privately, saying, Tell us, when shall these things be? and what shall be the sign of thy coming, and of the end of the world?
2. **Matthew 24:14** — And this gospel of the kingdom shall be preached in all the world for a witness unto all nations; and then shall the end come.
3. **Daniel 12:4** — But thou, O Daniel, shut up the words, and seal the book, even to the time of the end: many shall run to and fro, and knowledge shall be increased.

GREEK WORDS
1. "when" — ποτέ (*pote*): exactly when; indicates specific information
2. "what" — τι (*ti*): minute, minuscule detail; exactly; explicitly
3. "sign" — σημεῖον (*semeion*): a marker or a sign used to alert a traveler to where he is on a road; authenticating marks or specific signs
4. "coming" — παρουσία (*parousia*): a technical word used to depict the royal visit of a king or emperor or the arrival of one who alone had the authority and power to right wrongs and to set things in order
5. "end" — συντέλειας (*sunteleias*): the closure, the summation, or the wrap-up of the age
6. "world" — αἰῶνος (*aionos*): not the world itself, but the age
7. "earth" — γῆς (*ges*): the world; the physical planet
8. "preach" — κηρύσσω (*kerusso*): to herald a message by any means possible; to broadcast
9. "nations" — ἔθνος (*ethnos*): nations; ethnicities; ethnic groups; it also expresses the idea of different customs, cultures, and civilizations; it pictures people from every culture, custom, civilization, race, color, or

ethnicity in the world; all the various races and colors of human flesh; all the cultures of the world; all civilizations worldwide
10. "then" — τότε (*tote*): exactly then
11. "end" — τέλος (*telos*): the ultimate conclusion or climax of a thing

SYNOPSIS

The Lord so desires to see people get saved that He has promised in His Word that "…the grace of God that brings salvation has appeared to all men" (Titus 2:11 *NKJV*). That said, at some point in these last days, the very last person living that God knows will say *yes* to Jesus is going to repent and be born again into God's family. At that moment, the Age of Grace, or the Church Age, will be complete, and Christ will come to snatch His people from the earth. The preaching of the Gospel to all nations is the final sign we'll see before the end of the age.

The emphasis of this lesson:

The ultimate sign that the very end of the age and Christ's return is near is the preaching and heralding of the Gospel to all who are living in the civilized, sophisticated world. The technological advancements of our day have enabled the worldwide availability of the Gospel like no generation before.

A Final Review of Our Anchor Verse

After leaving the temple area in Jerusalem, Jesus and His disciples made their way up to the Mount of Olives. The crowds were now dispersed, and the beautiful panoramic view of the Temple Mount was in front of them.

> **And as he [Jesus] sat upon the mount of Olives, the disciples came unto him privately, saying, Tell us, when shall these things be? and what shall be the sign of thy coming, and of the end of the world?"**
> **— Matthew 24:3**

Once more, let's review what the disciples asked Jesus and the meaning of the six key words in this verse: *when, what, sign, coming, end,* and *world*.

The word **"when"** is the Greek word *pote*, and it describes *specific information*. It pictures *one seeking a concrete answer*. The disciples asked Jesus for very specific, concrete information regarding *when* the things that He had spoken of would take place.

Next is the word **"what."** In Greek, it is the word *ti*, which describes *a minute, minuscule detail.* The use of this word is the equivalent of the disciples saying, "Lord, don't be vague. Tell us *precisely* — down to the smallest detail — *what* the sign of Your coming will be."

We saw that the word **"sign"** in Greek is the word *semeion*, and it describes *a marker or sign to alert a traveler to where he is on a road* and let him know how much further he had to go to reach his destination. By using the word *semeion*, the disciples were saying, "Lord, tell us explicitly and precisely the sign we're going to see as we journey down the prophetic road to confirm Your coming and be assured that the end is near."

This brings us to the word **"coming,"** the Greek word *parousia*, which describes *the coming of the Lord.* Some argue that it is only used to describe Christ's Second Coming at the end of the Tribulation, which is sometimes called the Second Advent. But a careful look at the New Testament reveals that the word *parousia* is used to describe both the rapture of the Church and the Second Coming. It is a technical word used to depict the royal visit of a king or emperor or the arrival of one who alone had the authority and power to correct wrongs and set things in order.

When Jesus comes in the Rapture, it will trigger the day of the Lord, which is the seven-year Tribulation period when God's wrath will be poured out on the ungodly inhabitants of the earth who refused to comply with His righteous standards. From the time of the Rapture until Christ's Second Coming, the Lord will go to work righting all wrongs, putting things in order, and dealing with all His enemies.

Next is the word **"end,"** the Greek word *sunteleias*. Rather than describe the absolute end of everything, the word *sunteleias* describes *the closure, summation, or wrap-up of something.*

Lastly is the word **"world,"** which is a poor translation. Although it may seem to describe *the physical planet*, which is the Greek word *ges*, it is actually the word *aionos*, which describes *an age.* The disciples understood that the current age would run its course, come to an end, and give birth to another age. We know from Scripture that the next age will be the Tribulation.

When we put the meaning of all these words together and insert them into Matthew 24:3, we see that what the disciples were saying is, "Lord, tell us *exactly* and *specifically* when all these things will be. What will be the *authenticating road marker* to tell us where we are prophetically in time? And what will be the sign to indicate Your coming and that this current age is about to wrap up?"

The Signs We'll See Before Jesus Comes

It should be noted that about one-third of the Bible deals with prophecy, and much of it centers on the return of Christ at the end of the age. Jesus' last-days discussion with His disciples, which is often referred to as the Olivet Discourse, is recorded in three of the four gospels — Matthew 24, Mark 13, and Luke 21. Here are the 18 signs we've examined that Jesus said we will see as we make our way to the wrap-up of the age and approach the time of His coming:

1. **Worldwide deception**

2. **Wars**

3. **Rumors of wars**

4. **Commotions**

5. **Nations rising against nations**

6. **Kingdoms rising against kingdoms**

7. **Famines**

8. **Scarcities**

9. **Economic woes**

10. **Pestilences**

11. **Diseases**

12. **Catastrophic events**

13. **Monstrous developments**

14. **Signs from the heavens**

15. **Worldwide persecution**

16. The emergence of false prophets

17. Iniquity will abound

18. The love of many will wax cold

As you read through these signs, did you notice which ones are taking place in the world around you? You may even be realizing that all 18 of these signs are very present in today's world. Jesus said, "Now when these things begin to happen, look up and lift up your heads, because your redemption draws near" (Luke 21:28 *NKJV*). The closer and closer we get to the end, the more frequent, the more numerous, and the more intense these signs will become.

Sign #19: Worldwide Preaching of the Gospel

The final prophetic sign indicating that we are on the very cusp of the end of the age and the return of Christ is the *worldwide preaching of the Gospel*. This authenticating marker was spoken by Jesus in Mark 13:10 and in Matthew 24:14, where Jesus declared:

And this gospel of the kingdom shall be preached in all the world for a witness unto all nations; and then shall the end come.

Certainly this verse speaks of the roles of pastors, teachers, and evangelists. But it also encompasses the part each individual believer plays in sharing the Gospel with those God brings across our path, not to mention the financial and prayer support we provide to ministries that are spreading the Good News. Every time you tell someone about Jesus, you are helping fulfill Jesus' words in Matthew 24:14.

For an even deeper understanding of what Jesus is saying in this verse, let's examine the original Greek meaning of a few key words.

First, notice the word "preached." It is the Greek word *kerusso*, which means *to herald or preach a message by any means possible*. It could also be loosely translated *to broadcast*.

Next, notice Jesus said that the Gospel will be preached "in all the world." Some people have taken this to mean every single person in the world has to hear the Gospel before Jesus comes, but that is not what the original text says. This phrase, "in all the world," can only be used in one way. It is a compound of two Greek words that describes *the inhabited world* where people live in cities, towns, and villages all over the earth. In Jesus' day, it referred to *the inhabited world* of the Roman Empire.

So when Jesus said that the Gospel will be preached "in all the world," He was prophesying that *the entire civilized, inhabited, sophisticated world,* or *the technologically advanced world* will hear the Good News before the end of the age and before He returns. In other words, wherever there is a civilization, a culture, or a society, the Gospel will be heralded, preached, and broadcast. This doesn't mean everyone will hear it, see it, or agree with it. It just means that at the very end of the age, the *availability* of the Gospel will be to the entire interconnected world.

Specifically, Jesus said that the Gospel will be "…preached in all the world for a witness unto all *nations*…" (Matthew 24:14). The word "nations" here is the Greek word *ethnos*, which describes *nations, ethnicities,* or *ethnic groups.* It also expresses the idea of different *customs, cultures,* and *civilizations.* Moreover, it pictures people from every culture, custom, civilization, race, color, or ethnicity in the world. Thus, it includes all the various races and colors of human flesh; all the cultures of the world; and all civilizations worldwide.

Jesus said that once the Gospel is available to all nations, "…then shall the end come" (Matthew 24:14). In Greek, the word "then" is *tote*, which means *exactly then* or *precisely then.* As soon as the Gospel is heralded and preached and made available to the entire civilized world, in that exact moment, the end of the age will come. This was Jesus' direct answer to the disciples' question in Matthew 24:3.

This brings us to the word "end," which is not the word *sunteleias* that we saw in Matthew 24:3. Rather, it is the Greek word *telos*, and it describes *the ultimate conclusion or climax of a thing.*

Putting the meanings of all these words together, we see that Jesus prophesied that at the very end of the age, just before He comes to rapture the Church, "The Gospel of the kingdom will be available and preached to all who are living in the civilized, technologically advanced world as a witness unto all nations, ethnic groups, cultures, and customs. At that precise moment, the ultimate conclusion of the age will come."

Technology Has Made the Gospel More Accessible Than Ever Before

Of course, the burgeoning media and Internet continue to expand the availability of the Gospel. This is a fulfillment of the prophetic words in Daniel 4:12, which says that at the time of the very end, "…Many shall run to and fro, and knowledge shall be increased."

In our fast-paced technological age, the information highway is overflowing. In addition to the efforts of missionaries, church evangelism, printed literature, and all kinds of radio and television programs, we now see the Gospel getting out exponentially through the Internet and social media outlets. The Good News is being disbursed on a broader scale than ever before in history.

Rick goes into more detail about this in his book, *Signs You'll See Just Before Jesus Comes*:

> **It has become nearly possible for the *whole world* to hear the message of the Gospel and the Kingdom of God — and to even hear it in many languages. As fast as the Internet is spreading across the globe, it won't be long until the whole world will be interconnected — with the possibility of reaching every people group.**
>
> **According to Jesus, the *last*, *greatest*, and *final* sign that we are at the very end of this present age is that the Gospel will be preached in all the world for a witness to the nations. Once this moment is reached, this present era will end as the Rapture occurs and the Church is evacuated from the earth.**
>
> **…In previous centuries, when missionaries started the arduous journey to their foreign-mission destination, they often packed their belongings in the casket they planned to be buried in. Most knew that it was unlikely they would ever return to their native soil.**
>
> **But today the proclamation of the Gospel is much different. Some ministers still pay the ultimate price of their lives to fulfill their heavenly assignments. But largely, heralding the Gospel is carried out through safer means.**

[In] my own ministry…we regularly do ministry face-to-face — and there is no replacement for that type of personal ministry — it is also true that for decades we have been broadcasting the teaching of God's Word over television and the Internet. Yes, we have conducted many massive crusades in which we have seen the lost saved and the sick healed. We have started churches, and we [oversee] a large church in Moscow [and many churches in the former USSR]. But much of our outreach has been through new and modern vehicles of communication. Every week, I reach [millions] of people through text messages, by phone, and through TV programs that are seen via terrestrial stations, satellite stations, and the Internet.

With all these amazing technological advances available for proclaiming the Gospel, there is still an enormous number of unreached nations and people groups that have never heard the Good News of Jesus Christ….

With all the advances being made in more sophisticated technology, this realization could happen very quickly. We are not so far from being able to address every nation and ethnic group with the Gospel — *in their own languages*. Also, because the use of the English language has increased in many places across the world, it is becoming less necessary for people to hear the salvation message in their native tongue.

…There are approximately [8.3 billion] mobile phones in the world right now…the population of the earth is about [8.1 billion]…Christian programming is available to most of this large percentage of people if they choose to watch or listen to it.

What's even more amazing to me is that there are thousands of TV channels in the world today that have the potential to carry Christian broadcasting in nearly every 'tongue' of the world, which is about [7,159] languages.

…These figures don't even include the inestimable number of shortwave radios owned by people all over the planet! Thus, it is easy to see that Christian programming is at least potentially available right now in many of these places.

> **Although there are…[several] billion people on the earth who have never heard the Good News of Jesus Christ, the Gospel message is having a worldwide impact and is penetrating thousands of these unreached people groups via communications technology.** *This means the end of this age is very near!* [1]

Indeed, the Gospel is available in unprecedented ways in every corner of the earth! And the moment its availability reaches the whole interconnected, civilized world, it will trigger the return of Jesus to rapture the Church and the close of the Church age.

In His immeasurable mercy and compassion, God is requiring the Gospel to be preached and heralded by all means to all inhabitants of the civilized world before this age ends and His wrath is poured out during the Tribulation.

Friend, we're living in a time when more people have access to the preaching of the Gospel and the teaching of the Bible than ever before. This is the ultimate prophetic sign screaming at us that the wrap-up of the age is almost here and Jesus is about to return for His Church. Our job is to preach and present the Gospel by any means to the whole world. Instead of drawing back from giving to missions, we need to continue supporting them with our finances and our prayers. There are people who still need to hear the Gospel.

Jesus gave us all these signs we would see before He comes not to scare us but to prepare us to live victoriously in these last of the last days. May you be encouraged, empowered, and equipped to be actively engaged in reaching others with the Gospel and prepared for His soon return.

STUDY QUESTIONS

> Study to shew thyself approved unto God, a workman that needeth not to be ashamed, rightly dividing the word of truth.
> — 2 Timothy 2:15

1. To help you know God's heart with regards to people hearing the Gospel and spending eternity with Him in Heaven instead of being separated from Him forever in hell, take some time to reflect on the following passages. Note God's heart for sinners and write down how you can begin to see people the same way.

- Ezekiel 18:23, 33:11
- Isaiah 1:18-19, 55:1-3
- 1 Timothy 2:1-4
- Titus 2:11-14
- 2 Peter 3:9

PRACTICAL APPLICATION

> But be ye doers of the word, and not hearers only, deceiving your own selves.
> —James 1:22

1. When Jesus gave the Great Commission — to go into all the world with the message of the Gospel (*see* Mark 16:15) — the believers in the Early Church took it very seriously. Are you serious about sharing the Gospel with people around you? In what ways are you actively involved in helping spread the Good News of Jesus (i.e., in your prayers, financial giving, and witnessing)?
2. With all the things that are happening in our world, it is clear that the end of the age is rapidly approaching, and eternity is just ahead. Jesus taught about eternity often, speaking about hell just as much — if not more — than He spoke about Heaven. As a Christian, why do you think it is important to never forget the reality of hell?
3. As you come to the end of these ten lessons on *How Close Are We To the End*, what is one of the greatest takeaways from this study that really impacted you? Why is this important to you?

---

[1] *Signs You'll See Just Before Jesus Comes* by Rick Renner — pp. 155-160

A Prayer To Receive Salvation

If you've never received Jesus as your Savior and Lord, now is the time for you to experience the new life Jesus wants to give you! To receive God's gift of salvation that can be obtained through Jesus alone, pray this prayer from your heart:

> *Jesus, I repent of my sin and receive You as my Savior and Lord. Wash away my sin with Your precious blood and make me completely new. I thank You that my sin is removed, and Satan no longer has any right to lay claim on me. Through Your empowering grace, I faithfully promise that I will serve You as my Lord for the rest of my life.*

If you just prayed this prayer of salvation, you are born again! You are a brand-new creation in Christ! Would you please let us know of your decision by going to **renner.org/salvation**? We would love to connect with you and pray for you as you begin your new life in Christ.

Scriptures for further study: John 3:16; John 14:6; Acts 4:12; Ephesians 1:7; Hebrews 10:19,20; 1 Peter 1:18,19; Romans 10:9,10; Colossians 1:13; 2 Corinthians 5:17; Romans 6:4; 1 Peter 1:3

Notes

CLAIM YOUR FREE RESOURCE!

As a way of introducing you further to the teaching ministry of Rick Renner, we would like to send you FREE of charge his teaching, "How To Receive a Miraculous Touch From God" on CD or as an MP3 download.

In His earthly ministry, Jesus commonly healed *all* who were sick of *all* their diseases. In this profound message, learn about the manifold dimensions of Christ's wisdom, goodness, power, and love toward all humanity who came to Him in faith with their needs.

☑ YES, I want to receive Rick Renner's monthly teaching letter!

Simply scan the QR code to claim this resource or go to:
renner.org/claim-your-free-offer

WITH US!

 renner.org

- facebook.com/rickrenner • facebook.com/rennerdenise
- youtube.com/rennerministries • youtube.com/deniserenner
- instagram.com/rickrrenner • instagram.com/rennerministries_
  instagram.com/rennerdenise

Dear Friend,

If you enjoyed this study guide and believe others would benefit from reading it, please leave a review on Amazon and recommend it to others — or *consider sharing a copy with a friend or loved one!*

There is a great need for *"teaching you can trust"* among God's people.

Your friends in Christ and for His Gospel,

Dirk & Denise Brinner